YOU'LL NEVER WALK ALONE

LIVERPOOL
FOOTBALL CLUB

EST·1892

THE OFFICIAL
LFC FAMILY
ALBUM

Produced by Sport Media for Liverpool Football Club
in association with
www.liverpoolfc.tv

Produced by Sport Media:
Executive Editor: Ken Rogers Editor: Steve Hanrahan
Production Editor: Paul Dove Art Editor: Rick Cooke
Sub Editor: Roy Gilfoyle Editorial Assistant: James Cleary
Designers: Barry Parker, Colin Sumpter, Lee Ashun,
Glen Hind, Alison Gilliland, Jamie Dunmore, James Kenyon
Writers: Chris McLoughlin, David Randles,
Gavin Kirk, John Hynes.
Sales and Marketing Manager: Elizabeth Morgan

ISBN: 978-1-905266-70-8

Photographs: Trinity Mirror, PA Photos, John Cocks.
With thanks to all at www.liverpoolfc.tv
Printed by Broad Link Enterprise Ltd

LFC FAMILY ALBUM

"Don't talk to me about the so-called
glory years at Anfield.
Look at what we've just won.
These are the glory years."

**– JAMIE CARRAGHER,
speaking after Istanbul, 2005**

Produced by Sport Media for Liverpool Football Club
in association with
www.liverpoolfc.tv

'PROBABLY THE MOST
IMPORTANT GOAL
I'VE SCORED IN MY
CAREER'

STEVEN GERRARD LIVERPOOL 3-1 OLYMPIAKOS,
CHAMPIONS LEAGUE, DECEMBER 2004

I'm getting a lot of credit for that goal and it was very important
and probably the most important goal I scored in my career but it's
only important because of Neil Mellor's goal and Florent Sinama-
Pongolle's goal.

That's definitely my favourite. Every time I hear Andy Gray's
commentary my hair stands up on my shoulders and neck and I get
goose pimples – and the same when I heard the commentary from
the radio with John Aldridge. It was a magic goal and I'm proud of
it.

To score important goals is brilliant. The buzz and feeling is there
with every goal but when it's more important you get an extra
feeling. These are the reasons why you play.

▶ www.liverpoolfc.tv/album/gerrard

STEVEN GERRARD 201

200 LFC FAMILY ALBUM

'MY ANSWER
WILL ALWAYS
BE THE
GOALS
I SCORE'

FERNANDO TORRES LIVING UP TO EXPECTATIONS,
LIVERPOOL 6-0 DERBY COUNTY, SEPTEMBER 2007

After I left Atletico Madrid I dreamed of days like
I had against Derby. It was a magic Saturday. My
objective now is to be an idol at Liverpool and if I
keep scoring goals like this then hopefully it will
help me become a favourite for the fans.

I know that many people have doubted me
because of the size of the transfer fee but my answer
will always be with the goals I score. That is the
most important thing in the world, especially for
me as a striker who feeds on goals.

Playing for Liverpool – and because of the
history and how successful they have been over the
years – there is always a pressure that you have got
to go out and win trophies.

▶ www.liverpoolfc.tv/team/squad/stats

FERNANDO TORRES 91

The family album that takes you from the pitch to the page to the web

BILL SHANKLY once famously said that he "wanted to build a family of people that can hold their heads up high and say: 'We're Liverpool'."

The Anfield family is still as strong as ever but the way we are recording the special moments in our club's life is moving with the times.

A giant army of Reds descended on Istanbul in 2005 – nearly all of them armed with digital cameras and mobile phones ready to record their own personal story of an unforgettable night.

So it is at Anfield. You may still have a video of that Steven Gerrard corner or a recording of the Fernando Torres song on your phone.

To ensure the LFC Family Album is the ultimate keepsake for the modern generation, we have teamed up with the club's official website to provide a web link.

On www.liverpoolfc.tv, you will find a section devoted to the LFC Family Album.

There you will see a menu of options providing you with 15 video clips from the extensive LFC archive plus up to date statistics for the players featured.

These clips link in with selected pictures in this book. Where there is live footage provided, you will see the video symbol (see below) and there will be a URL link www.liverpoolfc.tv/album/player that will enable you to access the video clip.

It means that the action carries on and enables you to recapture in full the magic of that special Anfield memory – from the pitch to the page to the web.

There are other official website links in this book that will be marked by a story symbol (see below). These include team and player statistics and features.

These are all designed to make your journey through Liverpool's colourful recent history all the more enjoyable.

 Website story link   Website video link

Don't forget – if you want to follow Liverpool every step of the way, you can subscribe to the official weekly LFC magazine by logging on to www.merseyshop.com

If you want to enjoy more video footage from selected matches over the past decade, subscribe to the e-season ticket on www.liverpoolfc.tv and take advantage of their comprehensive archive.

LFC FAMILY ALBUM CONTENTS

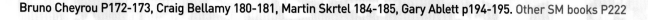

'IT WAS THE WORST PAIN OF MY LIFE BUT IT WAS WORTH IT'

JAMIE CARRAGHER CRAMP V AC MILAN, 2005

It brings a tear to my eye, but not because of the emotion of the occasion. I've broken my leg before and it's not nice, but the cramp I had was the worst, honestly. The pain was absolutely unbearable. I was lying inside our penalty area screaming for the physio to sort me out – it seemed like it took ages. Fortunately he patched me up, but even then I was always worried it might come back. It was the worst pain of my life – but you better believe it was worth it.

'I'LL HAVE TO BREAK
APPEARANCE
RECORDS INSTEAD'

**JAMIE CARRAGHER MAKING HIS 500TH LIVERPOOL
APPEARANCE V LUTON, ANFIELD, JANUARY 2008**

I love playing games. I want to play as many games
as I can. I'm not going to break any goalscoring
records, so I'll just have to try to break a few
appearance records instead.

www.liverpoolfc.tv/lfc_story/records

JAMIE CARRAGHER 13

'AS SOON AS YOU WIN IT YOU WANT TO DO IT AGAIN'

JAMIE CARRAGHER ISTANBUL

You don't think about it at the time, but you realise that people will look back on that moment and say that your career was a success, not least because the Champions League is so difficult to win. Personally, as soon as you win it you want to go out and do it again, as well as winning the championship, because that is what this club has been built on. Our predecessors won four European Cups before us and many championships and so we want to add to our honours list before we finish.

AC Milan's performance in the first half was from a different planet. They picked us off and were far too good for us. When I walked off at half-time, I just hoped it wasn't going to be five or six. People say that they still believed we could turn it round, but I didn't. I just didn't want it to be an embarrassment. There were a lot of heads in hands and everyone was devastated, but the manager made a few changes, we got an early goal and the rest is history.

▶ www.liverpoolfc.tv/album/carragher

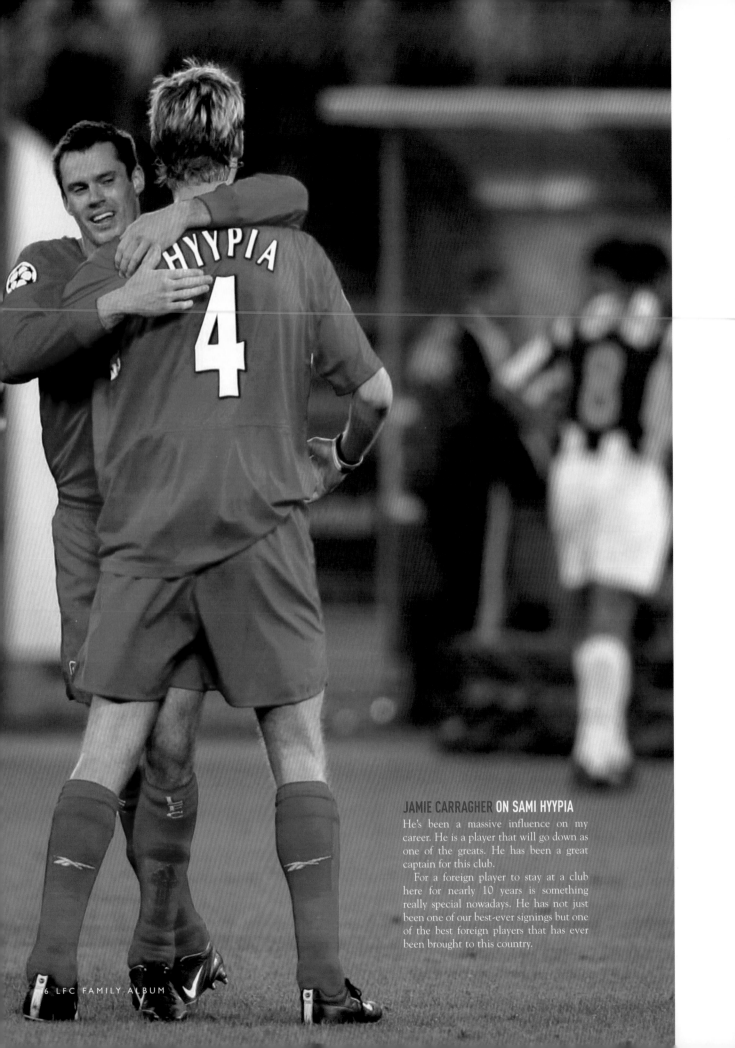

JAMIE CARRAGHER ON SAMI HYYPIA

He's been a massive influence on my career. He is a player that will go down as one of the greats. He has been a great captain for this club.

For a foreign player to stay at a club here for nearly 10 years is something really special nowadays. He has not just been one of our best-ever signings but one of the best foreign players that has ever been brought to this country.

JAMIE CARRAGHER GETTING 'STICK' FROM RAFA

I must have told the boss that Jose Mourinho's a better manager than he is in this picture!
He's actually probably giving me a bit of stick and telling me where I'm going wrong. He likes to do that.
He's always on the training pitch with the players every day. He's out there with you in all weathers in his shorts and
takes a very hands-on approach to the sessions. We, as players, respect that. There's a time and a place that you can have
a laugh and a joke with him, and that's great for morale, but we know when it's time to get serious.

'I LOVE THE EXTRA
RESPONSIBILITY'

JAMIE CARRAGHER WEARING THE ARMBAND

Captaining Liverpool at any time in your career is an
honour and doing it in the Champions League away
to Real Betis was great. We got a great win too to get
us off to a flier and it was nice to go through the
formalities before the game.

I love the extra responsibility of the captaincy but
it's Stevie's job and he does it brilliantly. I'm happy to
fill in when I'm needed.

www.liverpoolfc.tv/team/squad/carragher

'YOU FELT LIKE A PROPER FOOTBALLER'

JAMIE CARRAGHER A TASTE OF THE BIG TIME

This was the first serious football that I played. It was my first game with a representative team and we had corner flags, we had nets, we had referees and two assistants – the full works.

I'd only been playing Sunday League and the standard was mixed – this was my first taste up a level and it felt great. You felt like a proper footballer. I was the captain and Steven Rowan was the vice-captain. I was the centre-forward and he was the central defender. We were probably the two best players in the team then.

He was a good player at that level and I think he's still playing Sunday League.

JAMIE CARRAGHER LOSING TO AC MILAN, 2007

We got to another Champions League final and had some great scalps like Chelsea, but no one will remember that. It's about winning and that is what everyone at this club wants to do. It's all about winners.

I think we have to keep moving forward. Beating the likes of Barcelona and Chelsea gave us great confidence and we can take that into future seasons.

JAMIE CARRAGHER WITH REFEREE ROB STYLES, LIVERPOOL 1-1 CHELSEA, PREMIER LEAGUE, 2007

We just expect referees to come out and explain their decisions after a game. But that didn't happen afterwards and that created a bit of a storm. It's important that we move on. I was disappointed after the game and so was referee Rob Styles – that's why he came out on the Monday night and admitted he got it wrong. But what we don't want as players or as a club is to end up like Chelsea. Jose Mourinho was still banging on about Luis Garcia's goal in the first Champions League semi-final after the game two years after that incident and they couldn't get through a game against Liverpool without harping on about that. It's boring, to us and the rest of the country, and we don't want to wallow like that. Rob Styles is human, he made a mistake and it cost us two points.

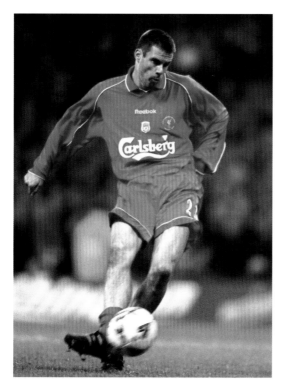

'I LOVE TAKING THEM. I TAKE ABOUT 10 EVERY DAY IN TRAINING'

JAMIE CARRAGHER SCORING IN THE PENALTY SHOOT-OUT V BIRMINGHAM, LEAGUE CUP FINAL, 2001

It was a bit disappointing for me because we'd allowed it to go to penalties. That was a game we should have won comfortably in normal time.

I wasn't nervous about taking a penalty because I enjoy doing it. I also think that if you miss a penalty it shouldn't be blamed on the person who misses – you should look at what you did or didn't do in the 90 minutes.

I didn't feel any pressure at all at the time; it's only now thinking about everything like the people watching in the stadium and at home.

I love taking them. I take about 10 every day in training and I'd love to get on them in matches because it wouldn't bother me if I missed – it happens. Plus it's a great way to get your goals tally up.

'IT WAS A ONE IN A MILLION THING'

JAMIE CARRAGHER WITH MATES AND FAMILY IN ISTANBUL

This was pure chance, and I'm not making it up. My cousin's at the front of the picture and my brother's trying to fight his way to the front too. It's just all my mates and family. It was a one in a million thing. I didn't know where they were before the game kicked off. I just went off on one and spotted them out of the corner of my eye. It just made the night all the more memorable for me.

JAMIE CARRAGHER CELEBRATING THE FIRST OF THREE TROPHIES IN 2001

I think this must be my trademark celebration now because there's a picture of me with Jerzy just after Shevchenko's missed the last penalty in Istanbul and I'm doing exactly the same as I am here at the Worthington Cup final. Every time we win something I seem to be doing a high-jump impression. I just hope I get to do it a few more times – after I've scored would be nice.

It probably gets overlooked what we achieved this season a little bit because of what eventually happened in Istanbul. When you actually think about what we achieved there, to win three different cup competitions is difficult. I mean, you can get knocked out by any team at any time in the cup and we played some great teams along the way, so it was difficult, but a great season.

'I THINK THIS MUST BE MY TRADEMARK CELEBRATION'

'IT WAS THE BEST FEELING.
I WENT A LITTLE BIT
BALLISTIC'

YOSSI BENAYOUN FIRST LIVERPOOL HAT-TRICK V BESIKTAS, 2007

It was amazing to score my first hat-trick for Liverpool Football Club. I never think about these things before the game. I never say to myself 'oh, today I want to score one goal, two or three goals.'

It hadn't crossed my mind that I might score a hat-trick for Liverpool. It just isn't something I'd thought about until it happened.

Even when I'd scored two goals against Besiktas here I was just happy with that. I wasn't thinking about a hat-trick.

You can see by my celebration here how delighted I was. The feeling was incredible. Once that third goal went in, that's when it struck me. I remember thinking 'wow, I've just scored a hat-trick for Liverpool and in the Champions League too!'

It was the best feeling. That's why I celebrated the third goal more than the other two and went a little ballistic about it.

A hat-trick is something special. You don't just have the memories but also get to keep the ball.

 www.liverpoolfc.tv/album/benayoun

'I THINK HE WANTS ME TO SPEND MORE TIME IN THE GYM!'

YOSSI BENAYOUN **TRAINING WITH RAFA**

I think the boss is saying he wants me to spend more time in the gym so I'm showing him exactly what I'm going to do!

I've had to toughen up since I came to the Premiership, there's no doubt about that. But I don't think it's a major problem for me any more. I'm able to handle the physical nature of the English league now.

That picture was taken during a training session on our trip to Hong Kong. The conditions out there were really tough. It was very hot which proved beneficial when we played in Toulouse.

The whole squad worked very hard during all of pre-season and it was really enjoyable. It helped us start the season well.

In terms of fitness work the training camp in Switzerland was similar to a lot of the pre-seasons I've done in Spain and at other clubs.

The major difference was on the tactical side – that was something I hadn't experienced before. It was new and it helped me to see why the boss has been so successful.

YOSSI BENAYOUN CARRA'S OWN GOAL, FA CUP FINAL 2006

I think everybody mentioned that game when I came to Liverpool,
although Jamie hasn't said too much about the fact that he put the ball in the net.
In the picture it looks like I've scored. When we went 1-0 up it was a really good feeling.
I was just a couple of yards behind Carra but I'm pretty sure I wouldn't have got to the ball before Pepe Reina.
To be perfectly honest in important games like that it doesn't really matter who finds the net.
As you can tell from my reaction and the look on Dean Ashton's face we were just happy to be ahead.
We enjoyed the goal celebrations with our fans but unfortunately it wasn't us taking the trophy home.
It was still an enjoyable occasion and one I will always look back on as a special memory.
Cup final day is famous all over the world and to have been a part of it was great.
The noise and colour inside the stadium really helped to create a great atmosphere and
both sets of supporters were fantastic. I thought we'd done it until Stevie intervened.

'IF I DIDN'T KNOW BETTER I'D THINK DIRK WAS A QUALITY DEFENDER'

YOSSI BENAYOUN WEST HAM 1-2 LIVERPOOL, PREMIER LEAGUE, JANUARY 2007

If I didn't know better I'd think Dirk Kuyt was a quality defender judging by this photo.

We had a decent side at West Ham but it was always really difficult to play against Liverpool. They beat us every time, even when we took the lead at Anfield, and of course in the FA Cup final.

This was another tough night. We really needed the points but they blew us away right at the start of the second half.

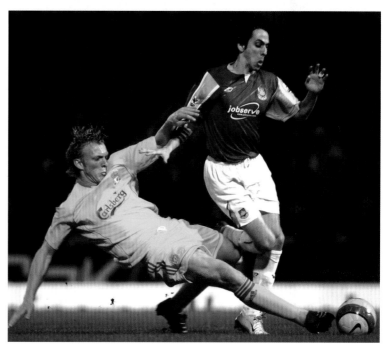

'YOU DON'T HAVE TO BE STRONG PHYSICALLY TO BE STRONG ON THE PITCH'

YOSSI BENAYOUN ON THE ENGLISH GAME

We scored just moments after this.

The ball ran free to Alonso and he put it away from the edge of the box.

I came on about half an hour from the end and Alonso scored his second goal of the match soon after.

I thought we should have had a penalty here. For me it was a foul, but luckily the ball came to Alonso and he scored anyway.

I remember when I went to West Ham people were asking me why I was going to England from Spain. It is much more aggressive here and they couldn't understand my decision.

I am not particularly big with a lot of muscles like some players, but I have always had confidence in my ability.

I'm not sure you always have to be strong physically to be strong on the pitch. For me, a lot of it is in the head. I'm not afraid to go into tackles or come up against bigger players. I can still win a lot of balls.

I'm not afraid of anything and think that I have proved myself in England, and that I can match the power and aggression here. The thing is to always work hard and continue to believe in myself.

www.liverpoolfc.tv/team/squad/benayoun

RYAN BABEL HANDS TO THE SKY, LIVERPOOL 4, ARSENAL 2, CHAMPIONS LEAGUE, 2008

I came on as substitute and I would often have that same impact and score goals (at my previous club Ajax) which led to people saying I was better from the bench. That was just in the beginning but in my last season I was starting every game. I missed maybe five or six games last season but in the ones I played I was having that impact from the beginning. It is just a question of time until I start to have that impact from the beginning of games with Liverpool.

▶ www.liverpoolfc.tv/album/babel

RYAN BABEL DEBUT DAY V CHELSEA, AUGUST 2007

I enjoyed the experience of that game. When I was getting warmed up on the sideline I was slightly nervous. The crowd was so loud and it was such a big occasion. I think this is the biggest league in Europe and to make my home debut during this fixture was special. When I got on and had some touches I settled down and hopefully showed the fans what I can do.

RYAN BABEL LEARNING FROM RAFA

My level has definitely improved since Ajax. I feel stronger and am more direct with my actions on the pitch. I have always liked to play from a standing position, with the ball played in to my feet when I am standing still and then I can take off. But already Rafa has told me to have more movement towards the goal as a way to preserve my energy for when I get the ball. I am learning these things all the time, which is helping my development.

www.liverpoolfc.tv/team/squad/babel

RYAN BABEL **33**

'I WILL SAVE IT FOR THE SPECIAL MOMENTS'

RYAN BABEL CELEBRATION SOMERSAULT AFTER SCORING V BOLTON, 2008

I think that was one of my better games for Liverpool and I felt more confident as the game went on. I am not where I want to be just yet but hopefully I will find my level and I can play beautiful football for Liverpool. I'm very happy with the goal because it was important that we scored the second to kill the game, so I am grateful for that. We kept pushing forward for the second and I always felt it would come, even though Jaaskelainen made some fantastic saves. So when I scored my goal I was really happy and that was why I celebrated like I did. But I won't be doing it all the time. I will save it for the special moments.

'I KNEW THAT THIS WAS MAYBE MY FINAL FAREWELL'

SAMI HYYPIA LIVERPOOL 2-2 CHARLTON, PREMIER LEAGUE, MAY 2007

It was a nice send-off from the fans, particularly as we had the Champions League final to come.

At this moment I wasn't sure what was going to happen over the summer. I knew that this was maybe my final farewell to the fans. Of course, I'm glad it wasn't.

At this time I didn't want to talk about these kinds of things before the final. Everybody just needed to concentrate on that game, including myself and the manager, so this wasn't the right time to talk about my future.

 www.liverpoolfc.tv/team/squad/hyypia

This is Roma's Marco Delvecchio. Maybe I said something to him for diving or something like that. Sometimes foreign players will try every trick in the book to get a free-kick. Personally, I don't like that kind of thing. That's not how I play football but I accept it. It is just part of their game and shows that they are willing to do anything they can to put you off and win.

SAMI HYYPIA BATTLE SCARS

I don't think I got that injury in this game – it was the one before. I'm sure it was Freddie Kanoute when he was playing for West Ham who caught me on the forehead with his elbow as we've jumped for a header.
I had stitches in my head for a few games after and that is why I needed something to protect me.
I still have the scar to remind me (laughs). This also brings back happy memories of playing alongside Stephane.
It was a good partnership and worked very well.

www.liverpoolfc.tv/team/past_players/henchoz

'ON THAT DAY I NEVER EXPECTED I WOULD WIN SO MANY TROPHIES'

SAMI HYYPIA SIGNING FOR LIVERPOOL

I am the only one of us left at the club. I had a lot of expectations here because I knew Liverpool was such a big club. I had always supported Liverpool when I was a little boy and it was like a dream come true to play here.

Nobody really knew me back then and so I could relax without too much pressure because nobody expected anything from me. This was a good thing for me in the first season and meant I could play my football and show people what I could do.

I've won everything possible with Liverpool other than the Premiership title, but on that day I never expected I would win so many trophies.

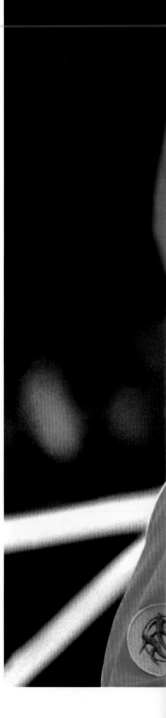

'WE DECIDED TO LIFT IT TOGETHER. IT WAS AN HONOUR'

SAMI HYYPIA UEFA CUP 2001

To win a trophy with Liverpool Football Club is a great thing, but to lift one as captain of the club was even better for me. Myself and Robbie Fowler lifted the UEFA Cup together here. He was vice-captain behind Jamie Redknapp, who was injured but I had been given the armband when Robbie was injured and so we decided to lift it together when he came back. It was an honour to hold the captaincy. It was a great thing in my life.

www.liverpoolfc.tv/lfc_story/2001.htm

'I WOULDN'T SAY SCORING
IS A HABIT'

SAMI HYYPIA SCORING V ARSENAL, CHAMPIONS LEAGUE, 2008

Up to that moment we hadn't played well but that brought us back into the game and gave us the confidence to go forward. I wouldn't say goalscoring is a habit. It's a bonus for me to score but I don't care who scores. I'd maybe prefer the strikers and midfielders to score and the defenders can look at keeping a clean sheet.

'AT HALF-TIME IN ISTANBUL
I WASN'T HAPPY'

SAMI HYYPIA THE PENALTY THAT NEVER WAS

At half-time in Istanbul I wasn't happy about the penalty Luis Garcia was denied. I saw the linesman signal to his hand as the officials were walking off the pitch so I was saying to the referee here that if the linesman saw it he should have given it. It's funny actually. I'm sure these three were the officials for Finland's game against the Czech Republic (later that year). It's definitely the same referee. He remembered me and we had a few more words during the game but not really anything about the final.

'YOU EITHER CRUMBLE UNDER PRESSURE OR YOU THRIVE ON IT'

MICHAEL OWEN THE WINNING GOAL, 2001 FA CUP FINAL,
LIVERPOOL 2-1 ARSENAL, MILLENNIUM STADIUM

If you play for Liverpool and England, and you're a striker, obviously you carry a lot of expectations. If loads of people are willing you to do well, then you either crumble under the pressure or you thrive on it. I'd like to think that I thrive on it. Everyone has a responsibility in the team. My main part is to provide goals and if I'm not doing that, I'm not doing my job.

MICHAEL OWEN 47

MICHAEL OWEN
DOUBLE AGAINST ROMA,
UEFA CUP, 2001

It changed my season. I was going through quite a bad patch at the time, so the game holds a special memory. We got drawn against Roma twice in consecutive years and we went through both times.

MICHAEL OWEN ON THE FANS AND LEAVING LIVERPOOL

I want to thank everyone at Liverpool – particularly the fans – for making my time there so memorable.
I was part of Liverpool since I was 11, and it will always be a part of my life.

'PEOPLE MADE A BIG DEAL OF THE FACT I WAS STILL ON 99'

MICHAEL OWEN 100TH GOAL FOR LIVERPOOL V WEST HAM, UPTON PARK, DECEMBER 29, 2001

2001 was a great year for me. I put my name alongside some of the great Liverpool strikers of the past who have scored 100 goals. It is a great honour for me and something I am very proud of.

People were making a big deal of the fact that I was still on 99 goals. But it was only three games since I last scored and it was never a worry for me. It was a great year for me with so many highlights: the goals against Germany, the goals in the FA Cup final and all the trophies that Liverpool won. It's the stuff that dreams are made of.

▶ www.liverpoolfc.tv/album/owen

'IT WAS A LUCKY GROUND FOR US'

MICHAEL OWEN SCORING THE SECOND GOAL, LIVERPOOL 2-0 MANCHESTER UNITED, WORTHINGTON CUP FINAL, CARDIFF, 2003

Certain grounds give you a buzz and it was a lucky ground for us. I was delighted for everyone that we won. The players took a bit of stick during that season so this was nice for everyone connected with the club.

My goal came from the first real chance I had. Against Arsenal it was the same scenario (in the 2001 FA Cup final), but you always have to be alive as a striker. When you have a back four as strong as ours you may as well make use of it.

www.liverpoolfc.tv/team/past_players/owen

ANDRIY VORONIN LIVERPOOL 2-2 TOTTENHAM,
PREMIER LEAGUE, OCTOBER 2007

Scoring any goal is always a special feeling; it
doesn't matter if it's a tap-in or a great strike. It's
pretty obvious I enjoyed this moment, particularly
in front of our own fans at Anfield.

Carlsberg

ANDRIY VORONIN 53

'I WANT TO BE THE BEST.
IT'S THE ONLY PHILOSOPHY I HAVE'

DANIEL AGGER SCORING AGAINST CHELSEA, CHAMPIONS LEAGUE, 2007

I want to be the best in everything I do. Of course, I need to work hard. I listen to everything that people tell me. Carra, the boss, Sami, other people. They all have experiences that I can use to make me better.

I want to win every game and a goal for me is the same whether I score from 30 yards against the best team in the league or from two yards against a reserve side.

If you have the mentality that one game is bigger or more important than the next then in the games that you don't think are as big you are not going to be able to always give 100 per cent.

That's not a place I ever want to go in my career. For me, I treat every game like I treated the final of the Champions League in Athens.

I want to make the most of my career, and this is the best way I know to do that. It is the only philosophy I have and I have no plans to change it.

www.liverpoolfc.tv/team/squad/agger

DANIEL AGGER ON MERSEY DERBIES

They are great games to be involved in and we felt that we had something to prove after the results against Everton in 2006/07. There is always a lot of physicality in this type of game and I enjoy that kind of test. I always enjoyed battling with Copenhagen in the derby back home. The fans get more excited, the players get more excited too and the game is played at 100 miles per hour.

'I'M NOT SOMEONE WHO LIKES
THE SPOTLIGHT'

DANIEL AGGER LIVERPOOL 2-1 WEST HAM, PREMIER LEAGUE, AUGUST 2006

I just wanted to go to the dressing room with my team-mates after scoring that goal but I had to do interviews. It's part of the game, although sometimes I'd rather avoid it. I'm not someone who likes the spotlight. If I could let somebody else do the interviews I would. I love to play football and that's why I'm at Liverpool. I'm not here to be in the media. I'll let others do that.

▶ www.liverpoolfc.tv/album/agger

'JAMIE CARRAGHER IS THE
BEST TEACHER
ANY YOUNG PLAYER CAN HAVE'

DANIEL AGGER ON A TOP CLASS TEAM-MATE

Jamie Carragher is the best defender in the world, and not only this, he is the best teacher any young player can have.

It's impossible for me to describe the level of respect I have for him and the way he's helped me in every game.

'ONE OF THE FANS LOOKED ACROSS AT ME AND SAID: 'RAFA, RAFA BENITEZ''

RAFA BENITEZ ONE NIGHT IN LEVERKUSEN

We went out to see the Champions League game between Chelsea and Barcelona. We couldn't see the game in the hotel so Alex and Pako said 'let's go out to a bar.'

We arrived at half-time and it was full of our fans. I started watching the game and one of the fans looked across at me and said 'Rafa, Rafa Benitez.' He started them all off singing 'Ra-fa Benitez...' Then they were all taking pictures with their mobile phones.

It was a fantastic atmosphere to be in amongst the supporters. I never did get to see the game after all but it was very funny.

'MY BROTHER WOULD BE AT THE DISCO. I WOULD BE TRAINING WITH THE BALL'

RAFA BENITEZ DOING KEEPY-UPS

This is the day before the Champions League final (in 2005) and I'm out with the players doing a light warm-up. Sometimes I like to enjoy myself with the ball. The problem at my age though is that you can't always do the things you want to and afterwards you realise you are not so fit any more. When I was young, about 18, I could keep the ball up many times. My brother would be at the disco with his friends but I would be training with the ball.

www.liverpoolfc.tv/team/squad/benitez

RAFA BENITEZ THE FANS

The fans are amazing. The atmosphere (against Arsenal in the Champions league, 2008) was incredible again. We know how their support helps us on nights like this. We were talking about it in the changing rooms before kick-off and at half-time and all of the players wanted to win it for the fans as much as anything else. They are very special.

RAFA BENITEZ WHAT HE DID TO CHANGE THE GAME IN ISTANBUL

It was very difficult to go into that dressing room at half-time and see the players with their heads down.
We talked about different things. We had worked very hard for 10 days and we needed to fight to the end.
You have to keep believing in yourself. We had fought hard to be in the final. I was thinking about what to say and what
to change. I needed to change the system and we needed to be more aggressive. I had to give confidence to the players.
The first thing I did was explain the plan to Didi. I wasn't thinking about winning then, only about scoring.
If we did that then Milan's reaction could be very different. They were afraid and everything changed when we scored.
I was last in the dressing room. I didn't hear Milan celebrate but Alex Miller did.
He told the players they were celebrating winning the cup. That was a good thing for us.

www.liverpoolfc.tv/lfc_story/2005.htm

'I WAS PLAYING AS A MIDFIELDER
OR SWEEPER'

RAFA BENITEZ 'TERRY MAC' AT 22

I am about 22 years old here – it must have been around
1982. I was playing as a midfielder or sweeper for Pajara, a
club based on the outskirts of Madrid. They were in the
Second Division and were only a small club but with a
great atmosphere. I remember having lots of good team-
mates and stayed there for four years.

'IT WAS A SPECIAL GAME.
IT WAS IMPORTANT
WE HELD ON'

RAFA BENITEZ JUVENTUS 0-0 LIVERPOOL, CHAMPIONS LEAGUE QUARTER-FINAL, SECOND LEG, 2005

When you play against top sides there is always more passion and people seem to pay more attention to these games. We were 2-1 up from the first leg but had to get a result at the Delle Alpi to progress to the semi-finals.

Xabi had problems with his ankle and had been out for some time. Our medical team worked really hard with him in order to get him back especially for this game. We used him as a holding midfielder and played with five defenders. We changed the system and thanks to the position of Xabi we could keep the ball and stay strong in defence.

It was a very special game which saw a big tactical change for us. It was really important that we held on. Remember, we were winning 2-0 at Anfield in the first leg and then Juventus scored at the end to make it 2-1.

All they had to do was beat us 1-0 in Turin and they knew they would be in the semi-final. Juventus already had this experience against Real Madrid in the previous round so they were saying 'we can do it, we can do it.'

This is why we needed to change things and try to be as strong as possible in defence. With Xabi playing where we put him and the five defenders it worked well. We had some chances on the counter-attack, whereas Juventus barely had any chances at all.

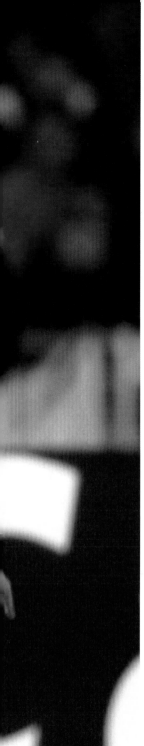

'KAKA WAS OUTSTANDING IN THE
FIRST HALF.
IN THE SECOND WE HAD A
BETTER SHAPE'

DIETMAR HAMANN SHACKLING KAKA, ISTANBUL

Kaka was outstanding in the first half but in the second half we had a better shape. They were 3-0 up and stepped down a gear – we shouldn't forget that. If they had carried on the way they'd played in the first half it would have been very hard to come back for us. If you want to come back at them from 3-0 down, everything has to be in your favour. They probably stepped down a bit, we played better football and won more challenges. They had a few near misses near the end.

www.liverpoolfc.tv/team/past_players/hamann

DIETMAR HAMANN DORTMUND, 2001

The UEFA Cup final in Dortmund. It was a great game. We were winning all the way and it went into extra-time. The Golden Goal decided the match. To win a European trophy in Germany was so special. We beat some great sides on the way to it; Roma, Olympiakos, Barcelona. It was a feeling of relief when Macca's free-kick went in off the defender.

DIETMAR HAMANN SWEET STRIKE

This was at Anfield against Portsmouth in 2004. Mike (Owen) played a great ball in from by the corner flag. He chipped the ball in and it came down about 18 or 20 yards from goal. I just caught it nearly perfectly in my stride with my left foot. It bent in a bit and ended up next to the post. The keeper didn't move. It was one of those you don't score too often.

'HE CAME BACK AND SAID 'YOU'RE FIRST''

DIETMAR HAMANN THE FIRST PENALTY IN ISTANBUL SHOOT-OUT

The manager asked me if I wanted to take one and two minutes later he came back and said: 'You're first'. I didn't really think about it but the good thing is it's done then and you can put it behind you. I was helped a bit by Serginho's miss so there was nothing to lose.

I just concentrated and picked my spot and fortunately it went in. He went to the same corner for every penalty so if I'd taken a later one it would have been harder. But if you knock them close to the post it's almost impossible to save.

▶ www.liverpoolfc.tv/album/hamann

'IT WAS SPECIAL WHEN I SCORED.
MY CELEBRATION
WAS FOR MY FAMILY
AND MY DAD'

**DIRK KUYT WINNING SPOT-KICK V CHELSEA,
CHAMPIONS LEAGUE SEMI-FINAL, ANFIELD, 2007**

I had quite a good feeling about everything going up to take my penalty because Pepe Reina had played a great game. He had a great day and had saved some penalties as well. All I had to worry about was shooting the ball into the back of the net – that was all I had to do.
I had no nerves at all really. I was actually nice and calm and I just picked where I wanted to put my kick and did it.

It was just so special when I scored and my celebration was for my family and my dad. I was thinking of how he came to all those games, the quarter-final and semi-final ties, and how we talked about them afterwards.

www.liverpoolfc.tv/team/kuyt

'I'VE MET EVERTONIANS WHO WEREN'T PLEASED.
IT'S NOT MY JOB
TO MAKE THEM HAPPY'

DIRK KUYT SCORING TWO PENALTIES AT GOODISON PARK,
EVERTON 1-2 LIVERPOOL, OCTOBER 2007

I'd only scored three times before that game but I had the confidence to step up for the two penalties. In my mind there was never any doubt about it.

Maybe it was a little strange (to take the second penalty) but I know what pressure is. I've dealt with it throughout my career. Situations like that are special.

I knew it was our last chance to win the game. There was only maybe a minute left so if I didn't score it probably would have finished 1-1. It's pressure but it's what you want to be part of. It gives you a buzz.

To win at Goodison Park in those circumstances was a great feeling. Avenging the previous year's defeat in that manner was special.

Since then I've met some people who were Evertonians and they said they weren't too pleased with me. We had a laugh about it. It's not my job to make them happy; only the Liverpool fans.

'IT'S IMPORTANT TO SHOW RESPECT BACK TO SUPPORTERS'

DIRK KUYT APPLAUDING THE FANS

I always go to the fans at the end of the game – at least I do when I score! I see it as respect for the supporters, as a way of thanking them for the incredible backing they give us. It was something I used to do at Utrecht and Feyenoord, because I like to thank them.

It's wonderful to play in front of supporters like these. They seem to respect me and I want to show the same for them at the end. Everyone has been really good since I arrived, trying to help as I settled in and it's important to show respect back to supporters.

Italian teams are very good in defence and Inter did really well, even with 10 men. But we remained patient and worked really hard together.

It was funny because just before I scored I said to Steven (Gerrard) that maybe we ought to keep the ball and keep the clean sheet.

But he said to me we needed to have another go and he was right because the goal came, we got a second and 2-0 is a great result.

It was a great moment (to score) because everyone knows how important it is to score a goal so I was really happy.

▶ www.liverpoolfc.tv/album/kuyt

DIRK KUYT CONSOLATION GOAL IN
CHAMPIONS LEAGUE FINAL, 2007

At half-time we were in control. We had a few little
chances and you have to be lucky to score a goal.
They were really lucky to score one minute before
half-time. We tried for 90 minutes but
unfortunately it didn't happen for us.

DIRK KUYT CHRISTMAS VISITS TO ALDER HEY HOSPITAL

I have experience of this hospital and I've been here a few times before. I know how good it is and how important it is for this area. They do wonderful things for these children. It's great that we can walk into the ward and help the kids forget about their problems for a while. They're happy to have the Liverpool players in their hospital with presents for them. It was good to have a chat with them and sign autographs. We came across a few Evertonians as well which was fun and we did our best to change them!

'LIVERPOOL FANS WILL ALWAYS
BACK YOU'

DIRK KUYT GOING THROUGH A STICKY PATCH

I truly believe I'm at the right club to help me whenever I'm out of form. The fans have been great to me. I think they understand what players go through.

At other clubs you might not always get that. The fans and the players all have the same targets; to win trophies and they help us to do that. It's a special feeling when you're not at your best and they still support you.

Every player loses form at some stage but Liverpool fans will always back you whenever you pull on that red shirt, no matter what.

We know we're lucky to have that and I want to reward their support and patience.

'I WAS ASKING GOD
TO PROTECT MY EYES'

MOMO SISSOKO THE EYE INJURY,
V BENFICA, CHAMPIONS LEAGUE, 2006

I was asking for God to protect my eyes. After the kick I knew
it was bad. Then I went to the hospital and they said the injury
was very serious. They said for a footballer it was bad and with
this injury it might be the end of my career. I was crying. I
couldn't sleep. There were a lot of things going through my
mind. It was difficult. I was only 21 and didn't know what I was
going to do for the rest of my life.

On the whole, I have to be happy simply because I can play
football again.

'I WAS DISAPPOINTED BUT I HAD TO BE FOCUSED'

XABI ALONSO BEING BOOKED AND MISSING THE CHAMPIONS LEAGUE SEMI-FINAL SECOND LEG, 2005

I was really disappointed at this moment. When I saw he dived I thought it could be a yellow card against Gudjohnsen. Then when the referee showed me the card I knew I would miss the second leg at Anfield. I was really sad but there were still 15 minutes left to play and it was 0-0 so I had to be focused. Afterwards, though, all I could think about was missing the second leg.

'IT WAS LIKE SOMETHING OUT OF A HITCHCOCK MOVIE'

XABI ALONSO THE PENALTY AGAINST AC MILAN, ATATURK STADIUM, MAY 25, 2005

Before the game Rafa told us that someone else other than Stevie would take the penalties and so when we got one I decided that I would take it. There was real suspense surrounding my penalty – it was like something out of a Hitchcock movie. I missed the first chance and then luckily the second one went in. I didn't have time to think about the miss as it all happened so fast. When I saw the ball hit the roof of the net I soon forgot about Alessandro Nesta's foul on me as I went for the rebound. It didn't matter any more.

www.liverpoolfc.tv/team/squad/alonso

'MY BEST AND WORST MOMENTS'

XABI ALONSO ON THE EUROPEAN CUP

What more can you say about the European Cup? It's a special competition that every player wants to win. Obviously it's not always possible and that's what makes it so good. The Champions League has given me my best and worst moments in football. Winning in 2005 was amazing. It doesn't get any better than that. But after losing in 2007 I was absolutely devastated. It's the most disappointed I've ever been following a defeat. Being on the pitch and watching AC Milan celebrating made me realise just how much I want to win this competition again. We had a great chance to make it two triumphs in three seasons but didn't take it.

XABI ALONSO SCORING FROM THE HALFWAY LINE. LIVERPOOL 2-0 NEWCASTLE, PREMIER LEAGUE, SEPTEMBER 2006

I practise it in every training session, but you have to try these things to make it happen. After I did it against Luton I was confident I could repeat it. I've tried it in a few games, and now I've been lucky enough to score. I was looking to pass to Stevie (Gerrard) but then when I looked up I saw the referee in the way of the pass and their keeper was well out of goal, so I gave it a try. Then I could hear the crowd shouting 'shoot' when I received the ball later, which was funny. But they will take away the element of surprise if I try it again!

▶ www.liverpoolfc.tv/album/alonso

'THE ATMOSPHERE THAT DAY
WAS RED HOT'

XABI ALONSO LIVERPOOL 2-1 ARSENAL,
PREMIER LEAGUE, NOVEMBER 2004

This is my first goal at Anfield. I remember the atmosphere that day was red hot. It gave me a great feeling to get my first goal. Then afterwards when Neil Mellor scored the late winner it was unbelievable. It was a great game to be involved in.

'THAT WAS THE BEST MOMENT OF MY LIFE UP UNTIL THEN, DEFINITELY'

JAY SPEARING MANCHESTER UNITED 0-1 LIVERPOOL ,
FA YOUTH CUP FINAL SECOND LEG, APRIL 2007

That was the best moment of my life up until then, definitely. To not be able to start in 2006 because of a broken leg, then to come back and captain the side and lift the trophy, that was a great honour for me. It was amazing to lift the trophy here. I'll always remember it and it'll always be in my mind.

www.liverpoolfc.tv/team/squad/spearing

'MY ANSWER WILL ALWAYS BE THE GOALS I SCORE'

FERNANDO TORRES LIVING UP TO EXPECTATIONS, LIVERPOOL 6-0 DERBY COUNTY, SEPTEMBER 2007

After I left Atletico Madrid I dreamed of days like I had against Derby. It was a magic Saturday. My objective now is to be an idol at Liverpool and if I keep scoring goals like this then hopefully it will help me become a favourite for the fans.

I know that many people have doubted me because of the size of the transfer fee but my answer will always be with the goals I score. That is the most important thing in the world, especially for me as a striker who feeds on goals.

Playing for Liverpool – and because of the history and how successful they have been over the years – there is always a pressure that you have got to go out and win trophies.

www.liverpoolfc.tv/team/squad/stats

'I HAVE NEVER FELT THAT BEFORE.
I WAS ALMOST
IN TEARS'

FERNANDO TORRES ATMOSPHERE OF PLAYING ARSENAL IN THE CHAMPIONS LEAGUE, 2008

The emotion I felt after the Arsenal game was very, very strong. I have never felt like that before. I was almost in tears at the end of the match when the crowd were singing. Without doubt, these have been the biggest matches of my career. I know football means so much and can give everyone strong feelings but it's still a new experience for me.

FERNANDO TORRES ON STEVEN GERRARD

When you play alongside a player like Stevie, it is easy to score like I have been. I am very comfortable with the partnership I have with Stevie and he is comfortable with me. We now must play like this for a long time together. We know where each other is running, where we are. I score, Stevie scores, and the team is winning. That is the most important thing.

**FERNANDO TORRES LIVERPOOL 4-1 FC PORTO,
CHAMPIONS LEAGUE, NOVEMBER 2007**

We knew we had to win and the way the match was turning out with the score at 1-1 we
were finding it hard to find a clear way to their goal. I feel the fans' affection, the support
from my team-mates and with each passing day I'm feeling more of a part of this and happier
with everything and at the end of the day those things are reflected on the pitch.

'WHAT I SAW AT ANFIELD THAT NIGHT WAS REALLY IMPRESSIVE'

FERNANDO TORRES ON RAFA AFTER THE FC PORTO MATCH

The atmosphere was amazing because of all that was going on during the
week with Rafa, and the people here really get behind the team when we
need their backing most.

It was great for those that had never enjoyed a night like this before and
especially for Benitez because we've seen that the supporters are really
behind him. I think Benitez is more than a manager. He's one of the greats
in their history and people feel that way about him and they show it.

We all had an idea that he's somewhat special here but, honestly, what I
saw at Anfield that night was really impressive. I'm really impressed at how
much he's loved by the people above anything else, even the players.

'I MOVED TO ENGLAND TO TEST MYSELF AGAINST
GREAT DEFENDERS'

FERNANDO TORRES THE FIRST
LIVERPOOL GOAL

I knew Liverpool games against Chelsea were special because the two sides have met each other so many times in the last few years. Because of that I was really looking forward to it and to score my first goal in such a big game was a dream come true. The atmosphere was spectacular and I really enjoyed it.

We did really well and were a bit unlucky not to take all three points. The Chelsea team have an excellent defence but we put them under some real pressure.

The battle against John Terry was also something I enjoyed. I moved to England to test myself against great defenders like that. It was my first for Liverpool and it came in an important game for us.

If you were to push me for my favourite moment so far then I would have to choose that one as being top.

▶ www.liverpoolfc.tv/album/torres

FERNANDO TORRES 97

'IT'S NOT ABOUT ME. IT'S ABOUT THE TEAM'

FERNANDO TORRES FIRST ANFIELD HAT-TRICK.
LIVERPOOL 3-2 MIDDLESBROUGH, FEBRUARY 2008

I didn't set myself a target at the start of the season. I just wanted to score as many goals as I could to make sure Liverpool were a success. It's not about me, it's about the team.

It was fantastic to score a hat-trick in front of the Kop. It was my first at Anfield and I felt very comfortable playing there.

www.liverpoolfc.tv/team/squad/torres

FERNANDO TORRES HOME

It's hard to explain. I just feel very at ease playing at Anfield. It's been like that from day one. For some reason many of my goals there have come in front of the Kop.

It just felt good from the start. I am very happy playing and scoring goals there. You try more things when you feel more relaxed.

Sometimes you just can't explain why you feel particularly good in a certain place but that is what has happened to me at Anfield.

FERNANDO TORRES SPAIN 4-0 UKRAINE, WORLD CUP, JUNE 2006

That looks like my team-mate Andriy Voronin lurking in the background. I must remind him of that game! We couldn't have started our World Cup campaign in better fashion. We played some great football on the day.

FERNANDO TORRES ON HIS CHANGING HAIRSTYLES

Everyone experiments with their hair when they're young, don't they? I certainly did. I still do, but not as much now that I've grown up a bit. This photo was taken at Euro 2004, although it doesn't feel like that long ago. I was just 20 and had numerous different hairstyles back then. I used to change it on a regular basis; it was just a bit of fun really. I think you should be allowed to do what you want. It's the same with the boss. A lot was said at first about Rafa's beard. The players gave him plenty of stick but he's still young so I don't see why he shouldn't be allowed to experiment too!

'I LIKE TO SEE THE PEOPLE'S FACES IN THE STANDS BEHIND THE GOAL'

FERNANDO TORRES SCORING

However I celebrate a goal just comes naturally to me. There is nothing I do which is special.

I like to see the people's faces in the stands behind the goal. It is great to see their faces and how they are celebrating and enjoying the moment. It is a pleasure that arrives as a culmination of a whole week's effort and work, the hours put in on the training field. For me, scoring goals is what it is all about.

It can be a funny thing though. Sometimes you have to wait until you see the ball actually hit the net before you know you have scored, but you can normally tell by the noise and reaction of the crowd. It can depend on the type of goal. You might fall off balance or have your back to goal and so you can't always see it going in. The goalkeeper might get a hand to the ball or it might hit a post.

But you always know when it has definitely gone in by the reaction of the crowd. They always let you know. Then the enjoyment tends to last until the referee blows his whistle to restart the match. It always seems quite a long time and, of course, you want it to last forever.

There is no better feeling than scoring a goal. In football it is the best you can get.

'WHEN I SAW THE BALL GO UP AND UP I THOUGHT

'OH MY GOD, IT'S GOING TO BE GOOD"

LUIS GARCIA LIVERPOOL 2-1 JUVENTUS
CHAMPIONS LEAGUE QUARTER-FINAL FIRST LEG, 2005

I saw the ball go up after I hit it and I thought 'Oh, I did it well.' But Gianluigi Buffon is very tall and I thought: 'Maybe he'll get to the ball.' Then when I saw the ball go up and up, I thought 'Oh my God, it's going to be good.'

Nobody expected me to shoot. I think even I wasn't sure. When the ball came I could either shoot or control. I could have gone forward but then I thought 'I have to shoot.' That was the best I scored that season.

▶ www.liverpoolfc.tv/album/garcia

'I ALWAYS DO THE SAME CELEBRATION AND I WON'T BE CHANGING IT'

LUIS GARCIA THUMB CELEBRATION

I always do the same celebration and I won't be changing it because it is special for me and my family. I did it for the first time just after my son was born and I have been doing it ever since.

'I SAW THE BALL GO IN.
IT WAS A GOAL'

**LUIS GARCIA LIVERPOOL 1-0 CHELSEA
CHAMPIONS LEAGUE SEMI-FINAL SECOND LEG, 2005**

If you see the ball and the post, it looks over the line and I don't believe the ball has stopped yet. The foot has to arrive at the ball and the ball is not going to be in that position. At the moment I saw the ball go in, I just ran to the supporters. I saw the ball go in. It was a goal.

All the people were shouting but no-one came to me. Then I saw the linesman running and I went 'Okay, it's a goal.' I was like 'Oh my God, what have I done?' It was very good. We knew at that moment that if we didn't make any mistakes we would be in the final.

www.liverpoolfc.tv/team/past_players/players/garcia/index.htm

'I KNEW FROM THE SPLIT SECOND'
THE BALL LEFT MY BOOT THAT I HAD SCORED'

LUIS GARCIA LIVERPOOL 2-1 CHELSEA
FA CUP SEMI-FINAL, 2006

I knew from a split second after the ball had left my boot that I had scored. The fact that I scored it at the end of the pitch where our supporters were made it an even more special moment for me.

LUIS GARCIA III

'EVERYTHING ABOUT THE
EUROPEAN CUP
IS 'HUGE'

LUCAS BESIKTAS 2-1 LIVERPOOL, UEFA CHAMPIONS LEAGUE, OCTOBER 2007

This picture was taken at a training session before the first time I played in a proper UEFA Champions League game. I'd come on in the qualifier against Toulouse but to be involved at the group stages was even more special.

Unfortunately we lost to Besiktas in a really tough game where we had a lot of possession but didn't make enough of it.

I played in the Copa Libertadores back in Brazil and – while they are both massive competitions – the European Cup is definitely bigger. Everything about it is huge, including the television coverage, the attendances and the teams who regularly feature.

'I'D HEARD A LOT ABOUT THE KOP, PARTICULARLY ON EUROPEAN NIGHTS, AND IT CERTAINLY LIVED UP TO ITS REPUTATION'

LUCAS LIVERPOOL 4-0 TOULOUSE, CHAMPIONS LEAGUE THIRD QUALIFYING ROUND, SECOND LEG, AUGUST 2007

That was my Liverpool debut and also my first game at Anfield. For me it was very special and a memory that will always stick in my mind.

I'd heard a lot about the Kop, particularly on European nights, and it certainly lived up to its reputation. The atmosphere was great. It eventually finished 4-0 with Dirk Kuyt getting two goals at the end.

That's twice when I've come on that he's scored in the last minute. Maybe I bring him some extra luck.

www.liverpoolfc.tv/team/squad/leiva

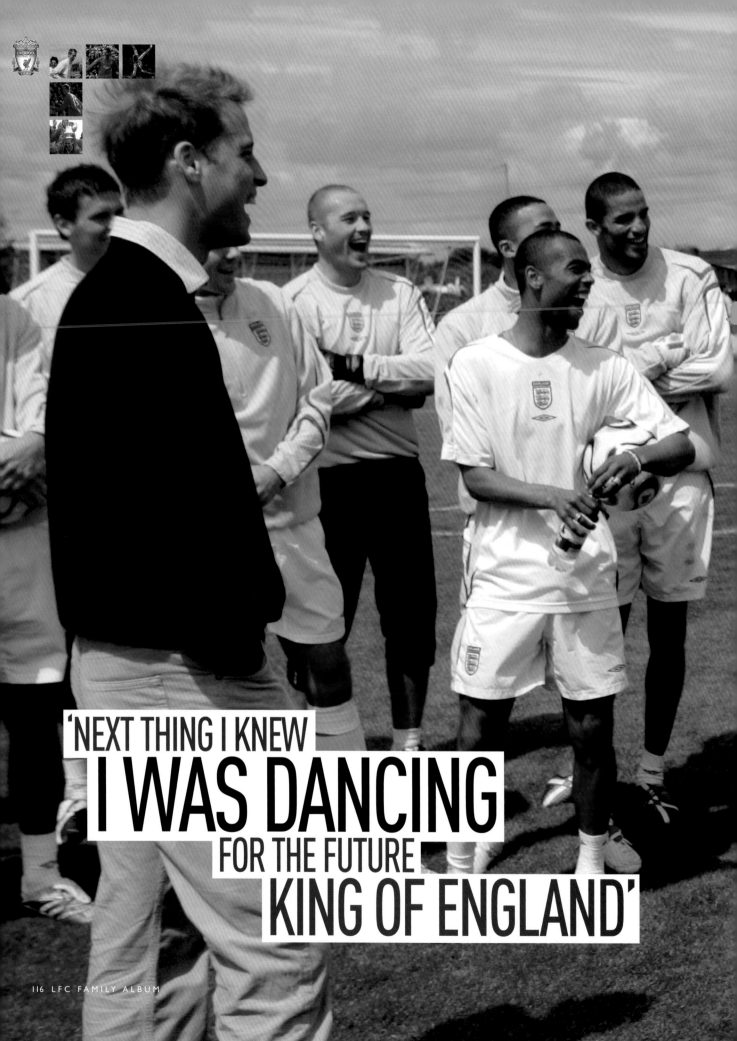

'NEXT THING I KNEW
I WAS DANCING
FOR THE FUTURE
KING OF ENGLAND'

I got goaded into doing it by a couple of the
lads and the next thing I knew I was dancing
for the future King of England. It was just
surreal. Did he like it? He seemed quite happy!

'GOALS FOR ME WERE LIKE BUSES
BECAUSE THERE WAS ANOTHER ONE ALONG A FEW MINUTES LATER'

**PETER CROUCH LIVERPOOL 3-0 WIGAN,
PREMIER LEAGUE, DECEMBER 2005**

That was a horrible, frustrating spell before I scored my first goal for Liverpool – it was too long, far too long before I found the net but I knew it was coming, I knew I'd get chances and I just had to keep confident. It was a massive relief, a great moment for me. Goals for me were like buses because there was another one along a few minutes later.

▶ www.liverpoolfc.tv/album/crouch

'IT WAS A SPECIAL MOMENT FOR ME TO SCORE THAT GOAL AT THE KOP END'

PETER CROUCH LIVERPOOL 3-2 GALATASARAY, CHAMPIONS LEAGUE, SEPTEMBER 2006

That was my best for the club. You don't get too many of those. It was a special moment for me to score that goal at the Kop end. Most of the time they go over the stand and thankfully that one went in the corner and it got us the win.

PETER CROUCH LIVERPOOL 1-0 MANCHESTER UNITED, FA CUP 5TH ROUND, FEBRUARY 2006

This was an important goal in a massive game. I knew about the rivalry between the clubs before I signed on at Anfield but I think it's only when you're there on the pitch that you begin to realise just how intense it is. I still remember just how much the place erupted after that one hit the back of the net. It made the hairs on the back of my neck stand up.

www.liverpoolfc.tv/match/season/2005-2006

'WE WERE ALL HANGING OVER THE EDGE OF THE BUS WATCHING THEM MAKE **THEIR GETAWAY'**

PETER CROUCH FA CUP HOMECOMING, 2006

My first homecoming celebration and a day I'll remember until I die. I've never seen so many people in my life and I was just buzzing for the whole day. Even when it rained the fans still sat patiently waiting for the bus to get to them. That's proper dedication.

We were laughing though because Luis Garcia and Didi Hamann sneaked off the bus at the top of the road that leads to Melwood and nobody noticed a thing. They were in disguise but they got away with it. We were all hanging over the edge of the bus watching them make their getaway.

PEPE REINA, PENALTY SHOOT-OUT HERO, FA CUP FINAL DAY, CARDIFF, 2006

Penalties are a real lottery and that day I won the lottery!

I was really disappointed with how I played over the 90 minutes. To be honest I was rubbish, absolutely rubbish. You just have to keep going.

The players thanked me for the save in extra time but that was only the same as I did to Stevie Gerrard after getting us the draw in the first place. That is part of my job and fortunately I have done that.

The next one (penalty taker) was Morientes and he said to me: 'Thank you very much, I didn't want to take one!' Before the penalties I wasn't praying, just talking to my friend in the sky and asking for some help.

PEPE REINA FEELING THE HEAT

It was warm when this picture was taken, and I must have needed
something to cool me down. So I made an ice cream for myself!

www.liverpoolfc.tv/team/melwood

'THE MANAGER'S TRAINING IS GREAT.
IT IS VERY DIFFERENT TO
TRAINING AT OTHER CLUBS'

PEPE REINA VICTIM OF THE CHASE

This picture was taken in the build-up to our home game with Besiktas in the Champions League and I think it shows you our relaxed frame of mind and the confidence we felt going into that game. It was vital to our qualification hopes but we were not too tense or worried about anything – as you saw from the 8-0 scoreline that was one of our best results in the first half of the season.

The manager's training is great. If you speak to the players they will all tell you the same thing – that it is very different to training at other clubs. Sometimes that can be important, because you don't want training to become too repetitive or become boring. As you can see from our faces here – it isn't at Liverpool.

'I REMEMBER SEEING MASKS IN THE STANDS AND THINKING THEY WERE INCREDIBLE'

PEPE REINA LOVES THE FANS

Our fans are unique. They go to the finals to give us their support but they make the whole experience much more special than that. They put time, thought and a lot of their hard earned money into coming all over the world to see us play football. This was a great example of that.

It was the FA Cup final in Cardiff and the fans had brought along massive masks of myself, Djibril Cisse and I think maybe there was one of Xabi Alonso too. I remember seeing them in the stands and thinking that they were incredible. It was an incredible game, and a wonderful comeback.

I missed out on the UEFA Champions League celebrations because I signed that summer, but I was able to be part of the tour around the city after beating West Ham and it was incredible.

The journey through the city took hours and hours to complete and we only travelled about six miles! Every corner that our bus turned I remember thinking that there could not be any more fans waiting for us – but of course there were! This is a special club; with special players and special fans. Between us there is a unique bond.

www.liverpoolfc.tv/team/squad/reina

'I WAS VERY NERVOUS BEFORE TAKING THE WINNING KICK'

MILAN BAROS LIVERPOOL HAT-TRICK, LIVERPOOL 3-2 CRYSTAL PALACE, 2004

Both were definite penalties in my eyes. We had claims for another one but the referee said no. Fortunately it didn't matter in the end.

I was very nervous before taking the winning penalty kick because I knew how important it was for us to win the match after the defeat we suffered in the game before against Birmingham. Of course, it was also the first time I scored three goals in a game for Liverpool. But the most important thing was that Liverpool got three points and we were all happy about that.

www.liverpoolfc.tv/team/past_players/players/baros

MILAN BAROS 129

'I WAS INJURED BUT I MANAGED TO RUN 50 YARDS TO CONNECT WITH THE BALL'

MARKUS BABBEL GOAL AT GOODISON PARK, EVERTON 2-3 LIVERPOOL, EASTER MONDAY 2001

It was fantastic. It was a very tough game for us at an important stage of the season against our big local rivals. It was important for the supporters and I knew that. I was injured when I scored the goal too. I was holding my leg and it was hurting, but I wanted to stay on for the team. I couldn't really run any more, but somehow I managed to run 50 yards to connect with the ball.

When the ball went in the net it was an amazing feeling. After the game all of the players went out, but I had to stay in because of my injury and receive treatment.

 www.liverpoolfc.tv/album/babbel

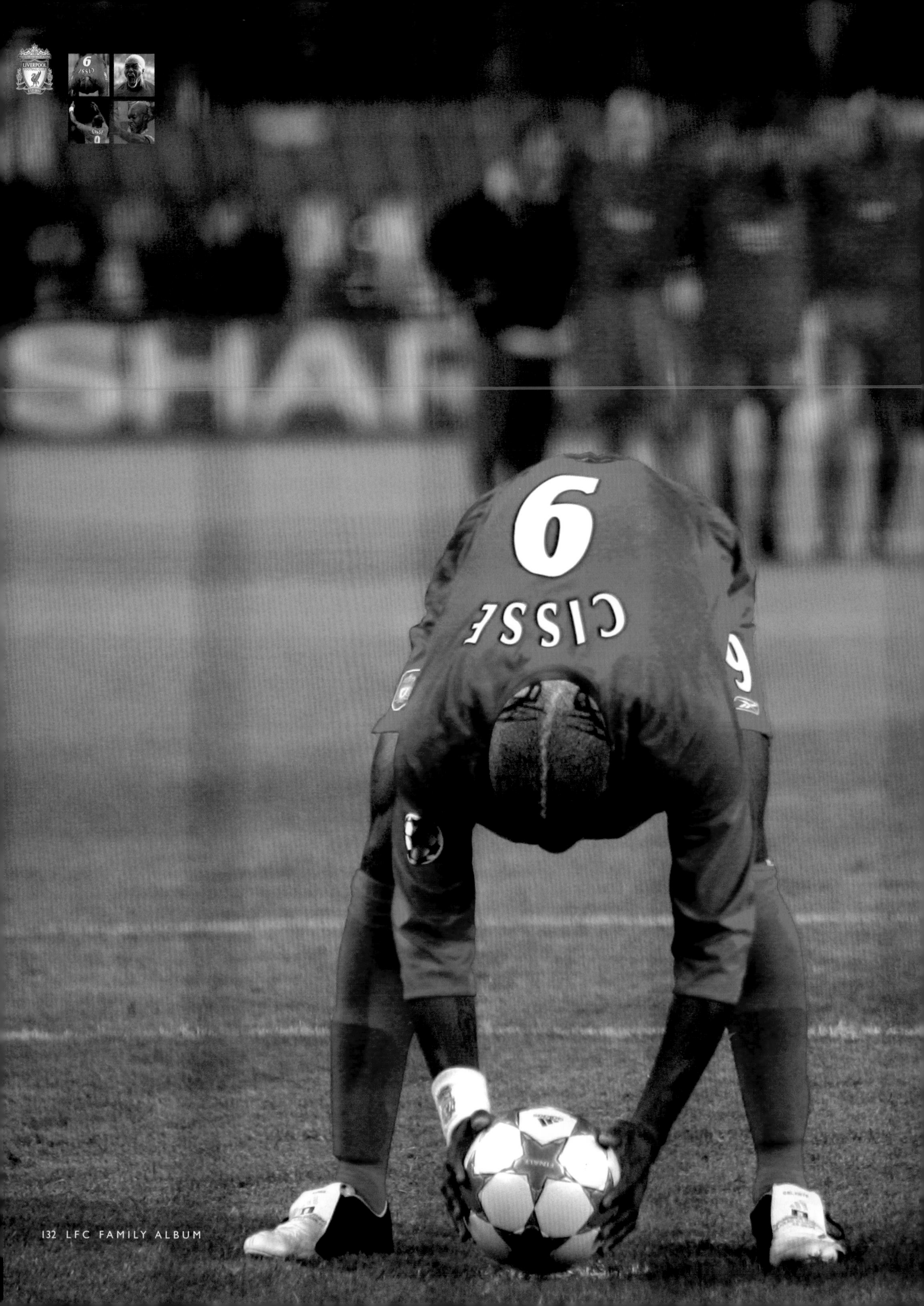
9
CISSE

'IT WAS LIKE TAKING A PENALTY WHEN YOU ARE A KID'

DJIBRIL CISSE LIVERPOOL 3-3 AC MILAN
UEFA CHAMPIONS LEAGUE FINAL, 2005

It was like taking a penalty when you are a kid. It's very exciting. I was not nervous at all, not scared. Six months earlier I was in my cast and on my crutches. For me it was special to be there and taking the penalty.

▶ www.liverpoolfc.tv/album/cisse

'I WAS A BIT ANGRY BECAUSE OF THEIR FANS SINGING ABOUT MY LEG'

DJIBRIL CISSE LIVERPOOL 1-0 BLACKBURN
PREMIER LEAGUE, OCTOBER 2005

It was really special because it was almost 12 months later, against the same team (as when I broke my leg). I was a little bit angry because of their fans singing about my leg but I am always happy to score goals, whether it's Blackburn or Chelsea; I don't care.

www.liverpoolfc.tv/team/past_players/players/cisse

'I WAS POINTING AT MY WIFE.
I WAS WAVING AT HER'

DJIBRIL CISSE LIVERPOOL 3-1 CSKA MOSCOW
EUROPEAN SUPER CUP, AUGUST 2005

I was pointing at my wife. I was waving at her. I scored two
goals within 20 minutes after coming off the bench in
France – my country. It was one of my best moments at
Liverpool, along with the Champions League.

DJIBRIL CISSE 137

'I WAS LOOKING AT
THE CLOCK
TO SEE HOW LONG WAS LEFT'

JOHN ARNE RIISE LIVERPOOL 4-0 FULHAM, PREMIER LEAGUE, DECEMBER 2006

It was towards the end of the game and I was looking at the clock to see how long was left. I think we were 3-0 up by this point. On this occasion there was a break in the game because someone was injured or a substitution was being made – that's why I'm almost sitting down here. At times like this I often get comments from the side of the pitch because I take the throw-ins on the left. I sometimes make a few comments back and have a laugh with the fans if there's a bit of a break like this.

JOHN ARNE RIISE BLACKBURN 0-0 LIVERPOOL, PREMIER LEAGUE, NOVEMBER 2007

It's always a tough place to play and we probably didn't perform too well, but still came away with a point and a clean sheet. Sometimes when I'm on the left near the dugout the manager will call me over for a quiet word. It might be something he wants me to change or it might just be instructions for one of the lads. It's easier for him to tell me rather than trying to shout over the crowd. On this occasion I think it was a message for Sami Hyypia. We knew their centre-half Christopher Samba would be a threat at set-pieces and he certainly was. They had a number of corners and free-kicks and he caused us some problems so the boss wanted Sami to pick him up.

JOHN ARNE RIISE LIVERPOOL 1-0 CHELSEA,
CHAMPIONS LEAGUE SEMI-FINAL SECOND LEG, MAY 2005

I didn't know what I was doing, it was just a reaction. It just happened and let's hope it happens again. To beat them at Anfield was just how we would have imagined it.

Everyone always mentions the amount of injury time that was added on that night. But before that I remember looking at the stadium clock. It said 89:44 so I thought there must be only two or maybe three minutes left. I've never, ever, been that tired. Then I noticed the board go up and six minutes flashed up. Unbelievable! I don't think I've ever seen one of those boards with that many minutes on it.

When the final whistle went the reaction was unbelievable. To know we were going to Istanbul was a special feeling, really crazy. Everyone was exhausted afterwards. The plan was for us all to go into town in our tracksuits but I was just too tired so I went home. I didn't have any energy left. I didn't feel that tired during the actual game but it was only when I sat down afterwards that it really hit me.

**JOHN ARNE RIISE LIVERPOOL 3-1 MANCHESTER UNITED,
PREMIER LEAGUE, NOVEMBER 2001**

That goal! I knew before the game that if a free-kick came up on the right-hand side I would be
taking it and I remember asking Didi Hamann to nudge the ball a metre and a half to the left.
It ran perfectly into my shooting stride and I made the perfect contact with the ball. I knew as soon
as it left my foot it was a good strike but to see it hit the back of the net the way it did was amazing.

www.liverpoolfc.tv/match/season/2001-2002

'SOMETIMES I WOULD COME OUT TO MY BIKE AND FIND MY SEAT HIDDEN'

JOHN ARNE RIISE CYCLING, DURING 2007 PRE-SEASON

This was an enjoyable part of pre-season when we went to
our training camp in Switzerland. We would take the bikes
down to the training ground every day, which was fun.
There was always a race to get there as we tried to beat each
other to see who could come first. All kinds of dirty tricks
were taking place to stop each other winning. Sometimes I
would come out to my bike and find the seat had been
hidden. I know Carra hid my seat a few times and he even
went as far as hiding my whole bike one day because he
didn't want me to win.

'I DIDN'T EVEN FEEL THE
CONTACT'

JOHN ARNE RIISE LIVERPOOL 2-3 CHELSEA, LEAGUE CUP FINAL, 2005

I hit this one so well that I didn't even feel the contact with my foot. You can see that Petr Cech hasn't even moved for it so it must have been an okay hit. I had actually been unmarked at the far post for about 30 seconds in the build-up to the goal because Paulo Ferreira had moved into the middle but the ball never arrived. When it did, I was only thinking about my technique and getting the ball on target.

VLADIMIR SMICER SCORING IN THE ATATURK STADIUM, MAY 25, 2005

When I think of the good moments at Liverpool I think of the winning goal I scored at Stamford Bridge against Chelsea. I think of the Michael Owen FA Cup final, the moment I actually realised my dream of signing my name on a Liverpool contract, winning the UEFA Cup and the Super Cup – I have so many happy memories.

I would feel like I had not been there for as long as I had if I was to be remembered only for that one night. It was a great goal though, and one of the ones I am most proud of.

I have never experienced anything in my life like a European Cup final. The main thing is in your head and the fact that you are playing for the biggest trophy in club football.

We were more relaxed, maybe too much so. I also think we paid the price for the fact that no-one in our team had played in a European Cup final, whereas Milan had much more experience.

When it's your first final it's very difficult. You can be too excited and start thinking: 'Oh my God, I'm playing in a European Cup final.'

Although we were 3-0 down at the interval, I felt we had prepared really well before the game. Normally you don't like to change your routine, but we went bowling on the morning before the final.

We could have gone for a walk in Istanbul but the players chose to do something a bit different. All of the squad took part and it was good fun and relaxed us.

I remember returning to my hotel room with Milan Baros after the match. The celebrations had finished and it was about six o'clock in the morning but I still couldn't sleep.

I ran the bath and was lying there until breakfast thinking about what had happened. The feeling of winning a European Cup cannot be bettered and a lot of times my mind goes back to that night. In fact, it's always in my head.

It was a long time since I scored a goal like that and, unbelievably, it was my first of the season so it was good timing. I celebrated with the largest cigar you have ever seen.

www.liverpoolfc.tv/team/past_players/players/smicer

'I RAN THE BATH
AND WAS LYING THERE
UNTIL BREAKFAST
THINKING ABOUT WHAT HAD HAPPENED'

'HE PUT HIS LIFE ON THE LINE FOR THIS CLUB'

PHIL THOMPSON LIVERPOOL 2-0 AS ROMA, GERARD HOULLIER'S RETURN FROM ILLNESS

Some people have said he came back a little too early but it was Gerard's decision. He loved the club so much that he wanted to come back when he did.

The game when he reappeared was another incredible night in the club's history. The players were so pumped up at Gerard returning.

He put his life on the line for the club and I hope people appreciated that. Gerard loved every minute of his time at Liverpool.

www.liverpoolfc.tv/team/past_players/managers/houllierobe

JERMAINE PENNANT LIVERPOOL 2-0 CHELSEA, PREMIER LEAGUE, ANFIELD, JANUARY 2007

To score a goal like that was very, very special and a great way for me to get my first goal for Liverpool. There was not much on for me in the box so I just thought I'd have a shot and it was nice to see it go in.

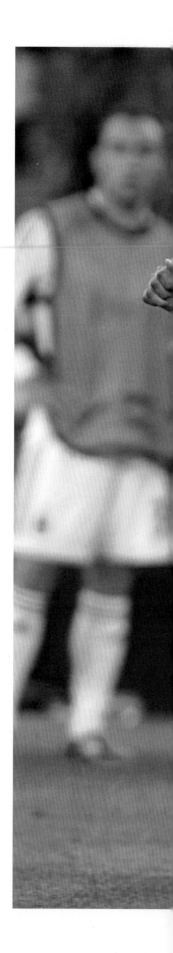

'TO GO FROM PRISON TO A CHAMPIONS LEAGUE FINAL WAS A MASSIVE TURNAROUND FOR ME'

JERMAINE PENNANT LIVERPOOL 1-2 AC MILAN, CHAMPIONS LEAGUE FINAL, MAY 2007

I've got no regrets about Athens. I think we gave it our all on the night and they got that little bit of luck that you sometimes need, especially with the deflection for the first goal right before half-time.

That's always a bad moment to concede and it was a real killer blow for us.

We were pushing for the equaliser and that suited them because they were able to hit us on the break.

But it was a great occasion and, despite the fact we lost, I still enjoyed playing in such a massive game.

I talked to my friends and family about how, just two years before, I thought my career was over.

To go from prison to a Champions League final in that space of time was a massive turnaround for me.

 www.liverpoolfc.tv/match/season/2006-2007

'HE'S BEEN EVERYTHING TO ME IN MY CAREER'

DANNY MURPHY ON GERARD HOULLIER

He's been everything to me in my career. At the time when he came, the club was going through a transitional period.

When he took sole charge he was the guy who sat me down and told me what I needed to do to get into the team. With his honesty and help, I've got to thank him for everything that I achieved.

He's a likeable guy and an honest person. If people are honest with you that creates respect.

www.liverpoolfc.tv/team/past_players/players/murphy

'COMING OFF THE PITCH AT MAN UNITED WHEN YOU'VE WON IS A FANTASTIC FEELING'

DANNY MURPHY MANCHESTER UNITED 0-1 LIVERPOOL, PREMIER LEAGUE, APRIL 2004

Old Trafford has been a very lucky ground for me, not just through goals. I made my England debut there. I played up front on my own and got man-of-the-match in 1998 (when Michael Owen was sent off) so that was a nice start to my Old Trafford 'career', if you like. It is such a fantastic arena to play in. People talk about the intimidation of playing in arenas like that, whereas I found it stimulated me. It was great to play in a stadium where the fans were so against you. Coming off the pitch at Man United when you've won is a fantastic feeling but coming off the pitch when you've won and scored the winner is doubly nice.

DANNY MURPHY EVERTON 1-2 LIVERPOOL, PREMIER LEAGUE, APRIL 2003

At that time of the season, in that game, it meant so much. Everton were above Liverpool and there was lots of talk about how they were doing better than us and the tide was turning. The cards were against us: Hyypia and Henchoz were both missing, Igor (Biscan) went off after five minutes, they equalised from a penalty, we were on the back foot. It just meant so much to so many people. Everton being the local rivals, with the stick that was going on at that time, that was special. It's nice scoring a free-kick or a penalty but that goal was a lovely one.

'I KNOW I CELEBRATED LIKE I HAD GONE CRAZY'

JAVIER MASCHERANO LIVERPOOL 2-1 READING, 2008
THE ARGENTINIAN'S FIRST LIVERPOOL GOAL

It was an incredible moment.

I had not scored a goal since I was back home in Argentina, so to score one for Liverpool – and in front of the Kop as well – was really special.

I cannot really describe the feeling but I know I celebrated like I had gone crazy. I can say that for those moments straight after the goal I did go a little bit crazy.

Some of the lads in the dressing room said I was like Inzaghi in the Champions League final!

It just meant so much to me and it was important also for the team because we had just gone a goal behind.

I would say never to expect the same number of goals from me that you get from someone like Steven (Gerrard). I do not have his vision or his shooting boots but I can say that I am working hard on this aspect of my game always.

I try to score goals in training. I really concentrate in shooting practice and I have been trying to get myself forward and more into positions where I can shoot myself or perhaps place a pass in front of another player for them to score goals.

All the time I try to improve and to get better.

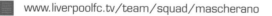
www.liverpoolfc.tv/team/squad/mascherano

'WHEN WE WERE LYING
ON THE GROUND
I THINK HE ATTEMPTED TO
BITE ME'

JAVIER MASCHERANO TOTTENHAM HOTSPUR 1-0 WEST HAM UNITED, PREMIER LEAGUE, OCTOBER 2006

Me and Edgar Davids were having a chat about an incident involving Jermain Defoe when we played Spurs at White Hart Lane last season. I'd tackled him from behind and it was a foul, but when we were lying on the ground I think he attempted to bite me. I was shocked at first and then a bit of a scuffle began with a few other players getting involved. I was trying to explain to Davids exactly what had happened but he didn't seem to understand what I was saying. Thankfully the situation calmed down pretty quickly although when I look back on it it was really strange.

'I NEED TO PROVE FOR EVERY MINUTE OF EVERY GAME THAT I HAVE A BIG HEART'

JAVIER MASCHERANO ON OVERCOMING HIS SIZE DISADVANTAGE

I am not as tall as Steven (Gerrard), or even as tall as any of the players that I play against so I need to be brave and prove for every minute of every game that I have a big heart.

I would say that in my position, because of my size, I have to try twice as hard as the opposition players I am playing against.

I am the smallest player in the Liverpool team. I am maybe one of the smallest central midfielders in the country and people will, I am sure, look at me before we play them and think that they will be able to dominate me physically.

I think that in the course of my time at Liverpool I have proved that they can't. I won't let them.

Sometimes it is hard when you have to challenge for headers with people who are almost twice the height that you are and go in for 50/50 challenges when they bring several stones more into the tackle.

That is why when I am asked who the toughest players are to play against for me in England I cannot choose one over the other.

Skilled midfielders playing for the top clubs are tough opponents for everyone to play against. However, playing against Derby or Reading can be just as hard for me because their players can be big and strong.

But I try my best, like I always do. I never pull out of a tackle and I think that commitment and determination overcome my size disadvantage.

England suits my style. You can go shoulder to shoulder with a player and give them a little bump here and there. In other countries touching a player can be enough to give away a foul.

That would make things more difficult for me and my game.

But I am so happy here.

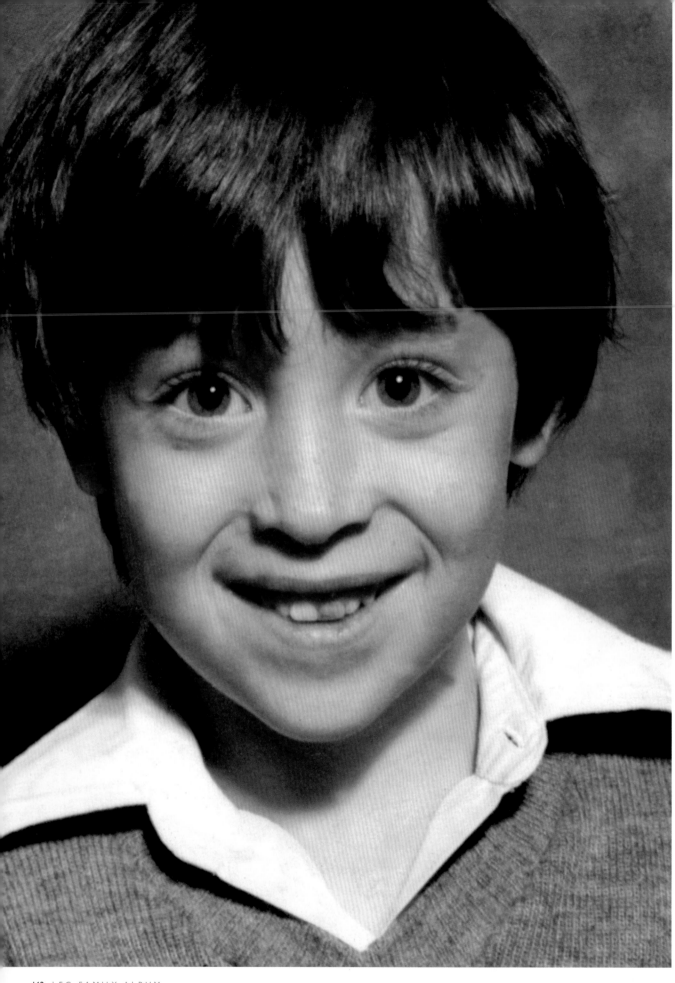

'I MUST HAVE BEEN FIVE OR SIX HERE.
MY HAIR MUST HAVE BEEN IN STYLE. IF NOT I'LL HAVE TO
REPRIMAND MY MUM'

ROBBIE FOWLER ST PATRICK'S SCHOOL PHOTO

I think the barnet (left) is back in style, isn't it? It's huge. I wish I had hair like that now.

It must have been the style then. If not I think I'll have to reprimand my mum.

I must be about five or six here. I wouldn't have been playing football then as I didn't really start until I was about 10. Yeah, definitely pre-football, thank God! I wouldn't have got too far with that head, would I?

ROBBIE FOWLER LIVERPOOL SCHOOLBOYS

I've got a bit of a cow's lick going on now.

I remember this well. It's with Liverpool Schoolboys and we were playing away against Wirral Schools.

The games always kicked off really early. This was taken at about half eight in the morning. From then until now I've always lacked a bit of sleep and I think this picture proves it. You can tell I've just woken up.

Looks like I've got the 'good ball' there too. There was always just one decent ball, none of the Mitre or Adidas that everyone uses now. Yeah, that looks like a Wembley Trophy to me!

'HAVING THE CHANCE TO BE INVOLVED IN THE CHAMPIONS LEAGUE FINAL AS A LIVERPOOL PLAYER AGAIN WAS SURREAL'

ROBBIE FOWLER BEING PART OF A
EUROPEAN CUP FINAL

Sitting there in the stands (in Istanbul), watching the game from a fan's perspective, I remember thinking the chance to take part in a game like that with Liverpool had well passed me by.

But just having the chance two years later to be involved in the Champions League final as a Liverpool player again was surreal to me.

'TO COME OFF THE BENCH AND GET A GOAL WAS SPECIAL'

**ROBBIE FOWLER LIVERPOOL 5 ALAVES 4 (AET)
UEFA CUP FINAL, 2001**

I hadn't started and that is what makes this such a sweet moment for me. It's always disappointing not to be playing in a final so to come off the bench and get a goal was special.

I was seconds away from getting the winning goal, too, but that wasn't to be once Jordi Cruyff equalised. Still, to get our hands on the trophy at the end was great. It completed the treble and got everyone buzzing again.

www.liverpoolfc.tv/lfc_story/2001.htm

'I JUST TEND TO JUMP AND GO A BIT MENTAL'

ROBBIE FOWLER SHEFFIELD UNITED 1-1 LIVERPOOL, AUGUST 2006

It was between myself and Craig Bellamy but I fancied it strongly and was pleased to see it go in as it pulled us back from 1-0 down. I think the celebration is the same one I've always done. I just tend to jump and go a bit mental.

www.liverpoolfc.tv/team/past_players/players/fowler

IGOR BISCAN ON THE ANFIELD CROWD

I don't know the reason for it but they have always supported me when I was playing badly and through the good times. I will always remember that.

'IT WAS AN INSTINCTIVE REACTION. I WAS SO HAPPY TO SEE THE BALL GO IN'

BRUNO CHEYROU HIS WINNER AT STAMFORD BRIDGE IN 2004

I always believe that hard work will pay off. It all happened too quickly. You don't think of what might happen. It was just an instinctive reaction. But it wasn't an easy chance because (John) Terry was just in front of me. I was so happy to see the ball go in.

www.liverpoolfc.tv/match/season/2003-2004

'ATTACK
HAS ALWAYS BEEN A
BIG PART
OF MY GAME'

STEVE FINNAN ON HIS BRAND OF FOOTBALL

I've always been a full-back who likes to push on. I'm a defender first and foremost but attack has always been a big part of my game. I want to improve on all of my game – attacking and defending.

It's natural for me to attack because I used to be a winger when I was younger, so I like to get forward and help the attack and try to set up goals. Obviously you don't let that affect your defensive duties but it is important as a full-back to get forward when you can and support the attack.

STEVE FINNAN ON CARRA AND STEVIE

Carra has played a lot of games for the club, like Stevie Gerrard. Carra and Stevie are two of the first names on the team sheet and they are good players to have alongside you; the type every good team needs.

STEVE FINNAN ON RAFA

You only have to look at the manager's CV. Judge him by the trophies he has won, and they show he is a top manager. He knows what he's doing. Rotation is obviously a subject that is raised a lot, and questions are asked, but it freshens up the squad and keeps players on their toes. If a player is unhappy because he is not playing, that's only natural because you want to play in a lot of games. But with so many games at club level, and with internationals, it could be over 60 games per season. The manager calls the shots and at a club like Liverpool, you are going to have to get used to it.

'IF IT HADN'T WORKED OUT I WOULD PROBABLY HAVE BEEN A BRICKIE'

STEVE FINNAN PLAYING IN A CHAMPIONS LEAGUE FINAL

I was at Wimbledon when I was 16. I was absolutely gutted to be released because, as everybody knows, at school you set your heart on something and when you are let down it is so disappointing. When I then went to Welling I had to think about the possibility of getting another job outside of football.

If that hadn't worked out then I would probably have joined the family building firm, working as a brickie or something like that. It is a big leap to be playing in the Champions League final – the biggest game of my career – but after what I've been through to get here, it holds no fears for me.

'WHEN I SCORED, I THOUGHT IT WOULD BE ENOUGH FOR US'

**JARI LITMANEN THE NEARLY MAN,
BAYER LEVERKUSEN 4-2 LIVERPOOL,
UEFA CHAMPIONS LEAGUE QUARTER-FINAL SECOND LEG, 2002**

All games teach you something. If you win it's natural to tend not to think so hard about what you can do better. When you lose, it can actually make you think more about things and consider in more detail what went wrong. Maybe there was something about our game which was missing in Germany.

When I scored, I thought that would be enough for us. I think we felt the same when Abel equalised. It was a very disappointing night. We had a good result in Liverpool and we hadn't lost away in Europe for such a long time – we expected a lot from the game.

We had good chances but you could see Leverkusen were a good side. They played great football. At the start it was in our hands but they scored the goals.

www.liverpoolfc.tv/team/past_players/players/litmanen

'I WAS GOBSMACKED.
COMING TO THE NOU CAMP WAS SOMETHING ELSE'

CRAIG BELLAMY BARCELONA 1-2 LIVERPOOL
UEFA CHAMPIONS LEAGUE LAST 16, 2007

All I wanted to do was make the most of the special atmosphere and the build-up to the game. I've been reasonably lucky in football, playing for my country and other big clubs, but this was my best moment.

It was important at the final whistle that we didn't milk the victory. The dressing room was actually quite subdued afterwards. Well, as subdued as it can be after a win at the Nou Camp.

It was a great result but it was only half-time. We had to go back to Anfield for a completely different game.

I was gobsmacked. Coming to the Nou Camp was something else.

'IT WAS LIKE A DREAM AND I'LL REMEMBER THE MOMENT FOR A LONG TIME'

NEIL MELLOR LIVERPOOL 2-1 ARSENAL
PREMIER LEAGUE 2004

The ball just dropped and I hit it, in front of the Kop in the last minute, against one of the top sides in Europe.

I went into it like any ordinary game. The lads and the manager were supportive of me and I came up with the goods. It was like a dream for me and I'll remember the moment for a long time.

▶ www.liverpoolfc.tv/album/mellor

'I DON'T KNOW HOW I DID IT'

JERZY DUDEK THAT DOUBLE SAVE FROM ANDRIY SHEVCHENKO

I don't know how I did it. Someone up there saved us. All I could do was prepare myself to make a save from the header and I managed to do that. Then he was straight up and it was obvious he was going to get the rebound. I jumped up as quickly as I could and made myself as big as possible and fortunately the ball hit my arm and went over the bar. I was waiting for this moment. That was by far the best and most important save I have ever made in my life.

'THIS WAS MY
REVENGE'

JERZY DUDEK LIVERPOOL 2-0 MANCHESTER UNITED
LEAGUE CUP FINAL, 2003

This was my revenge. I had a difficult time in the league game at Anfield and I had a chance to make amends to all the people who supported me through that bad time.

I got man-of-the-match for my performance at Cardiff but it was for everyone – the fans, the manager and the players.

It was a nice feeling, and it's the same any time we beat Manchester United.

www.liverpoolfc.tv/team/past_players/players/dudek

'I CAN HEAR THE SUPPORTERS CHEERING WHEN I GO IN FOR A 50/50 CHALLENGE'

MARTIN SKRTEL ENJOYING A TACKLE

I am a defender and sometimes that means you have to put your body on the line to prevent an opposition player scoring a goal.

I like tackling; it is one of my main strengths. And I can hear the supporters cheering when I go in for a 50/50 challenge. It's beautiful to me to hear that the Liverpool fans appreciate what I do.

It means a lot to me. To know that I have made an impact is pleasing because I am in a new country playing a new style of football.

The English style of play suits me very well. I enjoy physical battles with forwards and I have had plenty of those in England so far. I am sure over the course of my stay here at Liverpool, which I hope will be a long one, I will have many more.

www.liverpoolfc.tv/team/squad/skrtel

'I PUT EACH PENALTY EITHER SIDE OF THE KEEPER'

**FLORENT SINAMA-PONGOLLE TOTTENHAM 2 LIVERPOOL 2
LEAGUE CUP QUARTER-FINAL PENALTY SHOOTOUT, 2004**

This is the winning penalty. I got man-of-the-match that night and was very pleased. We had a really young team out but I was one of the most experienced players in the side. I was only 20 myself but it was a big, big game for me.

It was great to score two penalties in this game; one late in extra time to send it to penalties and then this one to win the shootout to get to the semi-final. I remember putting each penalty either side of the keeper. The first one went to the left and I put the second one to the right.

'THIS WAS NOT A POSED PICTURE. IT WAS NATURAL AND CAPTURED THE REAL EMOTION'

GERARD HOULLIER A HUG OF RESPECT

This was at the end of Macca's (Gary McAllister) last match for us. He had been a tremendous signing for us. This was not a posed picture. I prefer them like that because they are so natural and they capture the real emotion.

www.liverpoolfc.tv/team/past_players/players/mcallister

GARY ABLETT DEMANDING THE BEST, RESERVE CHAMPIONS, 2007-08

I would probably give them seven and a half out of ten for the season. Maybe that's slightly cruel but I can see a lot more potential to come from some of them. Hopefully next season they can fulfil that potential and break into the first team. There is always room for improvement. It's our job next pre-season to make sure we give them the right information and the right coaching to give them the best chance of moving into Rafa's plans. We achieved what we wanted to achieve in terms of winning trophies, but I want to see more of them playing first team games.

www.liverpoolfc.tv/match/reserves

'THE FEELING OF EMOTION WAS LIKE NOTHING I'VE FELT BEFORE'

STEVEN GERRARD LIFTING OL' BIG EARS & CELEBRATING ISTANBUL

A lot of us were sat in the dressing room at half-time with our head in our hands. We thought it was over. Milan played so well and so quickly in that first half that we were lucky only to be 3-0 down.

Rafa went over to the blackboard, got out his pen and started to make a few changes. He told us an early goal could change the course of the game, but I couldn't concentrate. All sorts of things were going through my head. It was just a weird, weird experience.

I suppose the first time I believed we could do it was in those last couple of minutes of extra time when Jerzy made that double save from Shevchenko. I think that was the moment when I thought that it might actually be our night.

Penalties were one of the tensest experiences of my life but the feeling of emotion afterwards was like nothing I've ever felt before. I was probably more grateful than anyone that Jerzy saved Shevchenko's penalty because I was next in line. I was on our fifth but my legs were dead and I could hardly walk, never mind shoot.

The celebration of that night is something I'll never forget and I remember promising that I wouldn't get drunk because you don't want to forget a detail. Celebrating with my dad and family in the team hotel was brilliant.

www.liverpoolfc.tv/lfc_story/honours

'HE MUST SPEND AGES PREENING IT'

STEVEN GERRARD **ON RAFA'S GOATEE**

He's taken a fair bit of stick from the lads since we turned up for pre-season training and were introduced to the goatee!

But fair's fair and the boss loves to give it out so he's got to expect to take a bit back for his whiskers.

He's always on the backs of the lads with long hair in the dressing room. Rafa will stand there watching them posing away, drying their hair and doing whatever it is they do with long hair. He'll wait until they've finished and then absolutely slaughter them. He gets plenty of practice because there are some real posers in our dressing room.

I'm probably home before some of them have finished sorting themselves out!

So the lads that have had to get used to taking loads from the boss have seen their chance to settle the score and they've gone for him mercilessly.

He takes it all in good spirit though, and it's great for morale that we've got the kind of manager that you can have a bit of banter with in the changing room.

I don't think he'll be too quick to judge this season because looking at his beard up close he must spend ages preening it and keeping it tidy.

'I WAS MORE INTERESTED
IN FOOTBALL THAN
THE LESSONS'

STEVEN GERRARD IN SCHOOL PHOTO

I was in third-year juniors. I was captain of the school team a year early. I used to love playing for the school. I was more interested in football than the lessons. I think that's why I never did too well at school! They were good days; I used to love them.

www.liverpoolfc.tv/team/squad/gerrard

STEVEN GERRARD LIVERPOOL 3-1 OLYMPIAKOS,
CHAMPIONS LEAGUE, DECEMBER 2004

I'm getting a lot of credit for that goal and it was very important
and probably the most important goal I scored in my career but it's
only important because of Neil Mellor's goal and Florent Sinama-
Pongolle's goal.

That's definitely my favourite. Every time I hear Andy Gray's
commentary my hair stands up on my shoulders and neck and I get
goose pimples – and the same when I heard the commentary from
the radio with John Aldridge. It was a magic goal and I'm proud of
it.

To score important goals is brilliant. The buzz and feeling is there
with every goal but when it's more important you get an extra
feeling. These are the reasons why you play.

▶ www.liverpoolfc.tv/album/gerrard

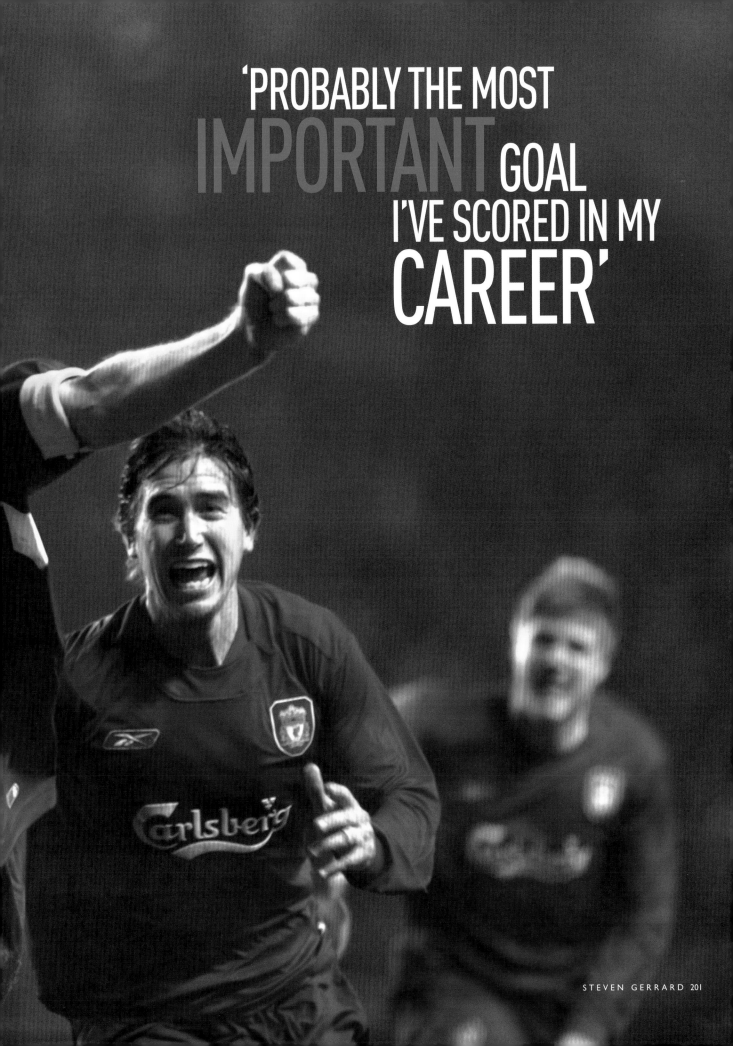

'PROBABLY THE MOST IMPORTANT GOAL I'VE SCORED IN MY CAREER'

'I KNEW AS SOON AS IT LEFT MY HEAD'

STEVEN GERRARD ON HIS ISTANBUL GOAL

My favourite goal has to be the header. I knew as soon as that left my head it was going into the net but I still watched it carefully just to be sure. The cross that came into the box was just in the perfect place for me. There was a bit still to do because Dida's a big keeper but there was plenty of pace still on the ball so it was more about guiding it into the corner.

'THERE'S NOTHING IN MY LEGS.
I CAN'T DO IT'

STEVEN GERRARD ON RECEIVING TREATMENT

I had absolutely nothing left, my muscles were tight. I can remember Benitez saying certain things, 'Do this and do that' and I was thinking 'Rafa, just go away because I've got nothing left, you can't ask me to do no more because I've got nothing left, there's nothing left.'

The manager said to me: 'The reason I've put you right-back is because we've had to bring Vladi on and Steve Finnan is injured. You've got the legs to play right-back and to try and stop Serginho.' I was that close to saying to him: 'There's nothing in my legs. I can't do it.' I just gave it a go and thankfully it worked out well.

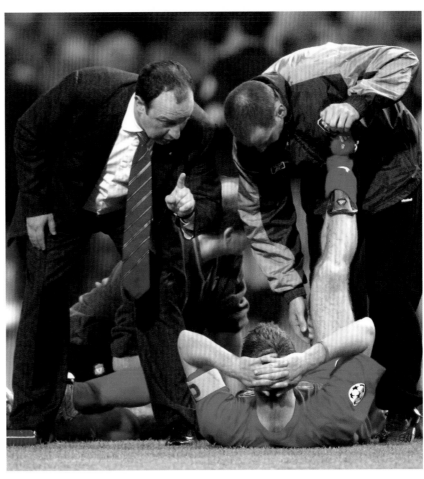

'I DON'T KNOW WHERE I GOT THE ENERGY FROM'

STEVEN GERRARD LAST GASP EQUALISING GOAL, LIVERPOOL 3-3 WEST HAM, FA CUP FINAL 2006

Just before my second goal I had taken a free-kick and it nearly went out of the stadium, my legs were so weary, so I don't quite know where I got the energy from.

I must admit I was absolutely delighted to hit the next shot like that. I didn't mean to put it exactly there but knew I had to get good contact to make sure it would hit the target and I caught it really sweetly.

It was a great moment when it went in, and I don't know how I did it. I just concentrated on giving everything to the shot.

I didn't hear the stadium announcer say how much extra was being added, but I knew there wasn't long left and it was really hard – I was all over the place. In fact, in extra time I just didn't want the ball. I just kept looking at the clock and wanting it to run out. I had absolutely nothing left.

We basically finished the game with about five men! People were going down with cramp all over the place, we'd put so much effort in.

The players were so brave because there were quite a few who would have come off if we had any subs left. We have a great team spirit here and we needed it to win that Cup. When it got to penalties we knew Pepe Reina would do it for us.

'TO LIFT THE FA CUP IS JUST AS SPECIAL'

STEVEN GERRARD ANOTHER 3-3, ANOTHER TROPHY, MAY 2006

Lifting the European Cup was the ultimate but to lift the FA Cup is just as special.

I've played in the final before but to lift the trophy as captain of Liverpool Football Club is a feeling I can't describe.

'I DIDN'T EVEN KNOW I'D BROKEN MICHAEL'S RECORD'

STEVEN GERRARD MARSEILLE 0-4 LIVERPOOL, CHAMPIONS LEAGUE, DECEMBER 2007

It was a fantastic result.

The manager told us that we'd need a cup final performance on the night and I think that's what we gave him.

You need a bit of luck to score goals and sometimes you get it and other times you don't.

I was glad to see the rebound go in because they would have got a lift from the keeper's save.

I didn't even know I'd broken Michael's (Owen) record (goals in European competition) until after the game. It wasn't something that was really that important to me before or during the game.

I'll probably look back on it at the end of my career and take a lot of pride from that and all the successes we've had.

'I LOVE PLAYING FOR THIS FOOTBALL CLUB'

STEVEN GERRARD LIVERPOOL 3-1 BLACKBURN, 300 LEAGUE GAMES FOR THE REDS

I wasn't really aware that this was my 300th league game until a couple of days after so it was a really proud day for me.

It only seems like recently that I made my debut so I'm really proud to clock up that many appearances.

I love playing football and I love playing for this football club. I've still got a load of goals, a load of ambitions and stuff to achieve here and that's what drives me on.

Obviously, I'd love to win the league and win more trophies.

Playing with top players and being coached by a top manager – that also drives me on.

'THE ATMOSPHERE THERE IS THE BEST IN THE WORLD'

MANUEL ALMUNIA LIVERPOOL 4-2 ARSENAL, CHAMPIONS LEAGUE QUARTER-FINAL 2008

For me, the atmosphere there (Anfield) is the best in the world.

Liverpool are great in the Champions League and if you aspire to be a great team then you have to be playing well in stadiums like Anfield.

You see the pure football at Anfield. The crowd and the team are as one together. The crowd lifts the team in any situation and that is fantastic.

www.liverpoolfc.tv/lfc_story/classics

'IT WAS A SILLY IDEA
THAT GREW INTO SOMETHING
THE FANS
COULD ASSOCIATE WITH'

'CARDINAL' MARTIN TSANG CANONISATION OF 'RAFATOLLAH' AND MARCH BEFORE BARCELONA GAME IN CHAMPIONS LEAGUE, MARCH, 2007

Once we got to Williamson Square it was really good. All of the supporters, including the Barca fans, really enjoyed themselves. They all wanted to touch The Rafatollah and pose with it.

When the canonisation was finished we went on a tour of the city. We visited The Cavern and a lot of the shops along Church Street. The whole day was brilliant. We did a few laps of the stadium where loads of people joined us.

The Rafatollah wasn't allowed into the ground due to safety reasons. We had to leave it with a friend of ours at reception.

This was a silly idea but it's now grown into something that lots of supporters can associate with. With that in mind, The Rafatollah will definitely ride again.

'IT WAS LIKE BEING ON THE KOP. IT TOOK YOUR BREATH AWAY'

BRIAN MOORE DRIVER OF THE BUS ON THE ISTANBUL HOMECOMING PARADE

When my boss said 'I'll let you drive the team bus' I nearly fell over. I've watched Liverpool since I was a kid and to be that close to them on that day was incredible.

When we got near Anfield I knew my family were all there but I couldn't see them. They were shouting at me but I couldn't hear them because the noise was unbelievable.

It was just like being on the Kop. It took your breath away.

THE FANS FERNANDO TORRES ON THE ANFIELD FAITHFUL

The supporters back the players regardless of who is out on the pitch. They enjoy watching their key players, because Liverpool has great players, but Liverpool will always be a team. The fans are always there until the death. That is the major difference with football back in Spain. If a team is not doing well, then it is because the players do not deserve to be wearing the club's colours. At Liverpool, if a player is wearing their shirt, it is because he deserves it. The fans ask for effort and dedication, and their support is something special.

ECHO AND THE BUNNYMEN'S IAN McCULLOCH THE TRADITION OF LIVERPOOL SONGS

The Ring of Fire chant cheers me up and it cheers the crowd up. Sometimes it doesn't matter what the song is or the chant, it's just the quickness of it and it's like one-touch singing. It lifts the players obviously and it lifts our fans but it also makes the opposition feel like...na, na, na, na, na! You know, that kind of mockery which is good as it gives you an edge in the game. Fans from other clubs are rubbish at it. In fact, they don't even try. They just stand there making noises and annoying you! That's how it's always been. At Liverpool it's like someone is passing on a baton to every half generation, and it's like, 'Come on, it's your turn now, give us a song'. It's great because during the course of the season that is one of the things that matters to us Liverpool fans. Instead of Goal of the Season, it's Chant of the Season or Tune of the Season.

'I WAS LUCKY ENOUGH TO BE AT THE AIRPORT WHEN ALDO ARRIVED AND GOT THIS
CRACKING PICTURE'

JIMMY PILNICK SPOTTING JOHN ALDRIDGE IN ISTANBUL, 2005

I was one of the fans lucky enough to be at the airport in Istanbul when Aldo arrived and managed to get a cracking picture with my mobile.

As for the game itself, what more can I say? I said beforehand I hoped Istanbul would be my generation's Rome 77. It was certainly that! And to come back the way we did was just fairytale stuff. Whatever happens in the future, I'll wake up every morning knowing I was there the night we brought the big cup home for good.

'THE WHOLE MATCH WAS PLAYED IN A PERFECT ATMOSPHERE'

MARKUS STUDER DEPUTY CHIEF EXECUTIVE OF UEFA AFTER THE 2005 'GAME OF FRIENDSHIP' BETWEEN LIVERPOOL AND JUVENTUS

It was perfect.

Liverpool must be applauded for the way they handled the arrangements and the fans of both clubs understood the message.

There was not a hint of trouble in the stadium. There was a fantastic atmosphere and both clubs must be praised. It was a very successful night for European football.

The mosaic was a very nice gesture and the Juventus fans warmly appreciated it. The whole match was played in a perfect atmosphere and the night was handled in the right way.

'RING OF FIRE
WAS HAMMERED OUT
FROM THE TOP OF
PEOPLE'S VOICES'

ALLEN BAYNES THE JOURNEY TO THE ATATURK STADIUM, ISTANBUL 2005

We went by taxi, nine of us in two taxis. We left Taksim Square at about 5pm and it was like Wacky Races meets Ben Hur. We hurtled out of the city, a yellow river of taxis. They were in front, either side, behind. The only place they didn't get was on top of us, although that was close!

There were scarves, flags, hats, shirts, and bodies, hanging out of taxis. Ring of Fire was hammered out on taxi roofs, car horns or just from the top of people's voices. It was like a Johnny Cash tribute on wheels.

I don't know if it was the noise that drew people out of their homes, but the roads were lined by local people clapping, cheering and shouting 'Liverpool!' They were brilliant, but so were we.

www.liverpoolfc.tv/news/kop_views

LIVE
AND
BREATHE
LFC
24/7

 LIVERPOOLFC.TV

ALL THE BEST BITS OF LFC TV WHEN YOU WANT THEM

LIVERPOOLFC.TV
e-Season Ticket

WATCH THE OFFICIAL CLUB TV CHANNEL LIVE ON E-SEASON TICKET, OR PICK OUT THE BEST BITS TO ENJOY ON DEMAND.

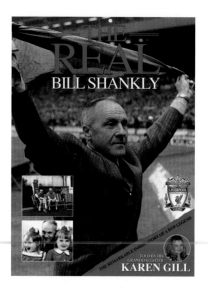

THE REAL BILL SHANKLY (paperback)

SEPTEMBER 29, 2006 marked the 25th anniversary of the death of the man who turned Liverpool Football Club from a struggling Second Division outfit to one of the bastions of world football. Bill Shankly was a remarkable character, but there were many sides to the legendary Scottish manager. Originally released as a best-selling hardback, this publication tells the inside story. THE REAL BILL SHANKLY provides a fascinating insight into the mind of this unique character through recollections from the fans who idolised him, the players who responded to his inspirational team talks and the family who loved him. The book is compiled by Karen Gill, the great man's granddaughter, who called him 'Grandy' while the fans called him 'The Messiah'.

There have been many Shankly books but this one, featuring marvellous photography from the unique archive collection of the *Liverpool Daily Post and Echo*, will be the definitive official record of his remarkable life – officially endorsed by Liverpool Football Club. It is a book every football fan will want to read. He was of an age when fans came before commercialism. Every single one of them mattered to Shankly.

Price: £14.99

THE REAL BOB PAISLEY

THE follow-up to the bestselling THE REAL BILL SHANKLY, this long overdue publication celebrates the life and times of arguably the most successful manager in British football history. It seems appropriate that at a time when over 40,000 people recently signed a petition to grant Bob Paisley a posthumous knighthood, his on and off-field life is examined and celebrated. The book offers an inside track, revelling in his life and times more than 30 years after he guided Liverpool Football Club to their first-ever European Cup triumph.

The complete story paints an accurate profile of a very private man through the eyes of his family, those who knew him the best away from the glare of the public eye. His treasured family album is made public for the very first time, while tributes from some of the game's greatest names only serve to enhance his reputation as one of the finest servants the English game has ever seen.

THE REAL BOB PAISLEY features marvellous photography from the unique archive collection of the *Liverpool Daily Post and Echo*, and will be the definitive official record of his life – officially endorsed by Liverpool FC.

Price: £20.00

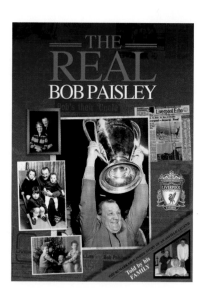

BILL SHANKLY: THE FORGOTTEN TAPES

JOURNALIST John Roberts was the man handed the immense honour of writing Bill Shankly's official autobiography in 1976.

Shanks was less than two years into retirement and still feeling raw as he wrestled with life outside Anfield. Roberts captured the Kop messiah's innermost thoughts on an old fashioned cassette recorder and these forgotten tapes, featured here, cover all the key aspects of his life.

This is the perfect opportunity to listen to the great man and be inspired again as he talks passionately about his time at Liverpool and discusses the special relationship he enjoyed with the fans as he took a struggling club to the pinnacle of European football.

Price: £9.99

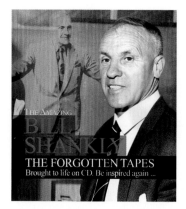

All of these titles can be bought by calling 0845 143 0001.

TOPS OF THE KOP: LFC KITS*

A FASCINATING look at the changing face of Liverpool's kit down the years. Every change is noted, taking into account developments in kit design and technology, variations in colour and of course the change in appearance of the famous red shirt, in the form of kit sponsorship.

Now updated to include the 2007-08 strips, the publication is supported by match action and iconic images (which bring the eras to life). It is an ideal companion to be used time and time again.

This beautifully-designed publication looks at the kit from 1892 to the present adidas era, through changes which included the change to an all red strip at the behest of the great Bill Shankly, who believed the players would look more imposing, more intimidating – and so it would prove as Liverpool FC swept all before them.

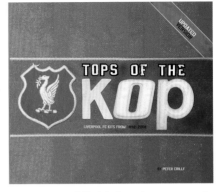

* Updated version now on sale

Price: £8.99

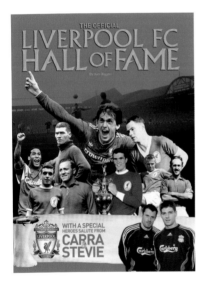

THE OFFICIAL LIVERPOOL FC HALL OF FAME

FIVE-TIMES European champions Liverpool Football Club have the richest history in British football. With such a prestigious heritage, the task for a specially selected panel of judges was how to select two iconic players for every decade from the many great players who have represented the club, in order to make up a star-studded official Hall of Fame.

This book provides the panel's answers, with some controversial decisions along the way. This is the definitive guide to the greatest Liverpool players of all time, illustrated with the finest archive photography.

In addition, the publication also reveals the name of every single individual who has played for the Anfield giants, with the 'Hall of Famers' themselves each having a dedicated statistical section.

It is written by Ken Rogers, former Sports Editor of the Liverpool Echo. He has also written the autobiographies of two Liverpool FC icons in Tommy Smith and Phil Thompson, and was co-author of *Liverpool – Club of the Century*.

Price: £20.00

LIVERPOOL FC: THE OFFICIAL GUIDE 2009

THE fourth edition of LIVERPOOL FC THE OFFICIAL GUIDE retains all the best elements of previous club yearbooks, while also utilising the expertise of club statisticians Dave Ball and Ged Rea to analyse further landmarks and records created during the 2007-08 campaign. Momo Sissoko netted Liverpool's 7,000th goal, Jose Reina created a new clean sheet landmark, Jamie Carragher made his 500th first-team appearance, further European records were broken while there was the 300th goal of the Benitez era, scored by Fernando Torres, who made such a big impact in his first season in English football.

Recognition of Liverpool's success in European competition and run to the Champions League semi-finals will be noted, while to mark the summer's European Championship finals, the record of Reds' players in the competition will also be noted. As ever, the aim of this publication is to make the yearbook relevant to fans all year round, be it with a useful club contact number, club fixtures, in-depth squad statistics or accurate club records to be utilised time and again. Available from October, 2008.

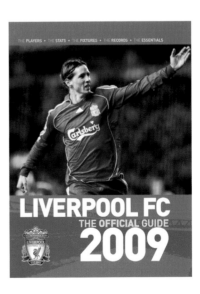

Price: £14.99

Or by logging on to www.merseyshop.com

YOU'LL NEVER WALK ALONE

LIVERPOOL
FOOTBALL CLUB

EST·1892

THE LFC FAMILY ALBUM